Looking For Love in All The Wrong Places

Ida Greene, PhD

Looking for Love in All the Wrong Places

ISBN 1-881165-05-1

Library of Congress Card Catalog Number:

ATTENTION COLLEGES AND UNIVERSITIES, CORPORATIONS, and PROFESSIONAL ORGANIZATIONS:

Quantity discounts are available on bulk purchases of this book for educational training purposes, fund raising, or gift giving.

For information contact: **P. S. I. Publishers, 2910 Baily Avenue, San Diego, CA 92105, (619) 262-9951**

.

CONTENTS

Looking For Love in All The Wrong Places

Introduction

These are my observations on who I am, and the factors that contributed to who I am, and my mother's impact on what I achieved or who I became. My mom only attended school to the 3rd grade, because she had to work in the cotton fields in Alabama to help the family survive. She could not read or write and made an "x" wherever her signature was needed. I taught my mom how to spell and write her name, Rosetta Green. My mom was so sad and disappointed that she could not go to school, that every day of my life when I heard the phrases "Get an education", "Get something in your head", I knew that was something no one can take away from you. "I wish I could have gotten an education," my mother said to me. "I would like one of my children to 'make something of them selves'." I heard the calling and took up her banner to get an education where I was given the freedom to be in yearly school plays.

I was involved in everything, traveling out of town to sing with the church choir, while at school I joined the Brownies/Girl Scouts and sold cookies. I joined a book club at age 12, got the family to take out a subscription to *LIFE Magazine*, which I found out later they could not afford but had wanted to support my desire for learning. We could not get my mom to go to night school to learn how to read, as she worked 2 jobs. Monday to Friday she worked in a hospital laundry room and on Saturday she cleaned houses for a white lady who was a Registered Nurse, which my mom hoped I would become one day—and I did.

My mom was so happy when I was on television at age 15; everyone sat around at home to watch me. All of my relatives in the city knew about it even though we did not have a telephone because we could not afford it. I am thankful to my mom, because she allowed me space to find myself, my talents, and find my many adopted mothers. I was emotionally adopted from the of age 6 by my many other mothers: my cousin and neighbor, Mama Coute; my 6th grade teacher, Ms Bascom; my neighbor and church member from Hauser Chapel CME church of Pensacola Florida, Mrs. Lee; my 9th grade teacher Mrs. Raglan; and my 10th to 12th grade teacher, Mrs. Dubose.

When I left home to attend Nursing school in Chicago I adopted a mother at my church, Bethel AME, Ms. Marie McArver, a single lady who never had children. When I arrived in San Diego at Bethel AME, I was adopted by a church member, Mrs. Veora Conley. Plus I had a cousin in Los Angeles, Mama Betty, my only family in California, and a cousin in Stroud Oklahoma, cousin Ella B. Argrow, who adopted me as her daughter into the Todd family of my grandmother, Adelle Todd Green, who died when my father was 12.

All of these mothers helped me to arrive at the place where I am today. Things my mom said to me: "It is a poor dog that does not wag its own tail (be proud of who you are). Always have your own money. Never ask anyone for anything unless you have to. Mama may have, Papa may have, but Spirit bless the child that's got her own. You can catch more flies with honey than you can with vinegar. (Be nice to people). Don't let your right hand know what your left hand is doing. (Keep some things to yourself, especially if it is something new you are starting and you are not sure how it will turn out). My mom always had some money tucked away. I never heard my mom ask my daddy for money, but I heard my dad ask my mom many times for money.

I realized later that my mom was the bread winner of the family, but the way she managed it, no one would have ever known. We always had to ask my dad for everything, even though she had the money. She made him feel like a man, because at that time in Florida black men had to say, "Yes Sir and No Ma'am" to all white people. Blacks and whites drank water at separate fountains, and we rode at the back of the bus. My dad was made to feel powerless outside our home; however, he was somebody in our home, because of my mom.

5

My mom vicariously graduated with me when I became a Registered Nurse, as well as when I got a BS in Psychology, an MS in Counseling, when I received my Pupil Personnel Credential to practice as a School Nurse/Counselor, when I received my Lifetime Teaching Credential in Psychology, when I received my degree and license as Marriage Family Child Therapist, when I received my Ph.D. in Psychology, and when I graduated from ministerial school with a Doctorate in Divinity. She witnessed me writing my first 4 books which she tried to help me sell to people in Pensacola.

Whenever I went home to Pensacola Florida to visit, my mom told the whole city I was coming home and I was treated like a celebrity. It was very humbling. The one time when I really knew that my mom loved and appreciated me for all I had done for her and our family was when she visited me in San Diego when I was working as a Registered Nurse. I never polished my white shoes, but my mom polished my shoes every day. She washed and laid out my work clothes on the bed for me before I went to work the 3-11 pm shift. I am so glad that I chose an uneducated woman who could not read or write, who worked 2 jobs except on Sundays, to be my mom. Her thirst for an education allowed her to pass her passion on to me. I love learning and achieving. I will be a continuous learner until the day I die. When my mom died in 1994 I had written 4 books. I now have 18 books. I can see both she and my dad in Heaven, smiling every time I accomplish or achieve something.

I will give you some ideas on how to find your true love and how to awaken the love lying dormant inside you.

Chapter 1
Facing the Inner Demon of Lost Love

If you have been single for a while and you are now ready to have a new love relationship, you can expect to have anxiety from your past relationships show up which can cloud how you enter into or approach a new relationship. You also may feel that finding that special someone will make everything in your life "better". If you spend your time and energy looking for your "better half" you will have feelings of inadequacy and incompletion. The odds are that you are doing things that are counterproductive to inviting love into your life. When you start to look for love you will need to clear away the emotional and physical clutter of your life to make room for love.

Another thing you will want to do is to let the lover or lost lover that "got away" go away. Do you feel that if timing or circumstances had been just a bit different your relationship would have worked? The strange thing about the past is that sometimes it can appear better from a distance. Maybe you have not taken the time to work through the hurt feelings and reasons why your lost love did not work. In order to move into a new relationship you need to let go of the things that did not work and focus your energy on what you are trying to achieve now. You may want to let go of the perfect boyfriend/girlfriend from your past. Take notice of what you liked about your past lover and remember it as a happy memory rather than as an impediment that will keep you in the past or keep you depressed and prevent you from moving forward. It paints a mental picture from your inner belief of who you think you can be, or what you believe you can have in your life.

Your self-esteem is a blueprint of who you are and how you have been treated, respected, appreciated, and identified by those around you. Your self-esteem is endless; it is the essence of who you are, not what anyone may see you as. It is fragile. It can be affected by many factors and needs continual maintenance. It reflects how you view yourself; how you honor, respect, and value yourself. It paints a mental picture or inner belief of who you think you can be in a relationship or what you believe you can do in your life.

Your self-esteem is the vehicle you use to move through life to achieve your goals. It is the package you create to get the things you want or to reach the goals you have set for yourself. Each person has a separate agenda, determined by what he or she is called to do in this lifetime. If your self-esteem is wholesome, and you feel good about yourself, you can accomplish great things. If your self-esteem is damaged, or less than what it could be, your ability to accomplish or achieve will be hampered by a negative self-concept. That negative picture will create a self-image that tells you that you are less than others, not good enough, that you cannot or will not be successful in your love life. We are each marching to a different drummer. Each person is unique and different. We need to see ourselves as kind, understanding, and powerful. Remember who you are is Spirit's gift to you, and what you make of yourself is your gift to Spirit.

We are all born to develop, create, change, and die. Nothing is static. Everything is in motion, a continuous energy transformation. We are born anew each hour. This is why it does us no good to hold on to the experiences of the past. If you rely only on your human ego, which is cold calculating, judgmental, and without feeling or compassion, you will experience needless pain and suffering.

A negative self-image reminds us continually that we cannot measure up to the standards of society. It matters not whether this is fact or fiction; if this belief held by an individual, it will hamper the contribution they make in life because they will be looking through a distorted mirror that will reflect a distorted image and message back to them that says, "I am different from others, I am not okay." Depending on our self-concept, self-belief, self-image, and self-respect, we will rise to great heights or fall to the depths of great despair. So let go of the notion that there is a perfect relationship or a perfect person you need to meet for you to be happy or find happiness in life.

There is no such thing as a perfect person or perfect relationship; besides perfect is a boring idea of what a relationship is or can be. I think it is helpful to write down the list of traits you want in a partner as well as deal breakers, but use this information a guideline to lessen your anxiety to start you on your journey to love and self-fulfillment. When you make your list of traits for what you want in a new lover and your deal breakers for the new lover, try to make sure that your list of qualities and traits addresses not just the surface traits like green eyes, brown hair, and chiseled features, but that it includes deeper qualities that address who they are as a person and who how they interact with others as couple or in a couple relationship. For example:

- Are they a morning person?
- Do they like to watch funny movies?
- What do they consider to be a romantic date?
- How do they like to spend a lazy afternoon?
- Do they like to share their emotions?
- Do they know how to have arguments in a healthy way?

Again, these lists are more for you to help tune your brain and heart towards being aware of the people who are a good fit for you. It is not to build a fortress of perfection that no one will ever be able to reach. Remember, all people have flaws, relationships are not perfect, and if you can allow for this ebb and flow of relationships to occur, it will make it much easier for you find a potential lover who is a good match for you. Be open to what the universe has to offer. You may find that the best surprises and connections arrive in a different package than what you expected.

Anyone can create a new image and increase our self-esteem by changing their thoughts about their self-worth, taking more risks in life, changing their thoughts and feelings on love, accepting that they are worthy and deserving of love, showing gratitude for the small ways love shows up in their life, avoiding feeling sorry for themselves when love does not show up in the way they would like, and taking small action steps to create a loving relationship. If you sit waiting for love to find you, you may be waiting for a long time. You will have to set yourself and your heart on fire with the passion of love so someone can see your flame. You do not need to grovel and allow someone to treat you without respect to be loved. Love is not abuse and abuse and disrespect are not love. These are some of the issues you need to look at so your self-esteem and self-worth are healthy and intact:

1. Ask for what you want without creating drama around your asking.

2. Take a risk, step out of your comfort zone, and relate in a genuine way, not as a victim wanting sympathy or pity.

3. Own what you are doing wrong. Are you playing the role of a victim? If so, is it because you do not feel you deserve better, or did you learn from your mom how to play a victim role? Is this is your role or purpose in life? Are unwilling to learn and grow for fear you will lose the people around you? Are you playing the role of a victim so others can love you, to have a family, to keep a family, to keep a husband, a child, or a lover?

4. Do not equate love with abuse and suffering.

5. Eliminate the feeling that love is long suffering

6. Be grateful for what you have.

7. Give up feeling no one will love you unless you let them treat you like the dirt on the ground they walk on.

8. Stop wanting others to feel sorry for how they treat you and when they don't, stop thinking you are getting what you feel you deserve and want.

9. Others will treat you the way you allow them to treat you.

10. When you make yourself a rug or carpet, people will walk all over you. Do not do it.

11. Do you love yourself? If not, why not?

12. Do you feel you deserve to be treated in a loving way?

13. Do you feel you deserve respect?

14. Where did you learn or who showed you how to be a door mat, to be treated like a slave, or like a "nobody"?

15. Do you have courage and do you take responsibility for the role you play in the way your relationships are unfolding?

16. Don't let others be responsible for your self-esteem, to be your jury, or to decide what happens in your life.

17. Everyone is responsible for creating their own joy, their love, their self-respect, their self-worth, their health, and the life they want to live.

18. You can be authentic and real, or you can be a victim.

19. You can stand up for yourself, or you can let others treat you as they want to treat you.

20. You can live like a peasant or a Queen/King, but you can't be both.

21. You can believe in yourself and work to improve yourself and your life. You can live with love, self-worth, and self-esteem.

22. Do you have the courage to love yourself even if you are the only one except Spirit who loves you?

We All Need the Following to Be Whole and Complete:

Security: Self-acceptance, a sense of belonging to someone or something.

Identity: Self-description to given you by your family of origin.

Support: Mental, physical, and emotional.

Desire: Dreams, visions, or goals.

Self-Esteem: Internal belief about yourself and the way you experience life. The five parts of self-esteem are self-concept, self-image, self-worth, self-respect, and self-confidence.

A. Self-Concept = Personal and Spiritual Identity
B. Self-Image = Inner picture of how you see yourself, reflects outside you
C. Self-Respect = Positive self-regard
D. Self-Worth = Importance to family, society, life (Spirit)
E. Self-Confidence = Self-assurance, comfort, inner peace

Spirituality: Your anchor, your purpose for living to contribute, and make a difference.

Aesthetic Appreciation: Non-human, a sense of awe and majesty.

We develop a sense of Security by having our birth and existence validated by someone other than ourselves. Someone, who by their words, actions, and deeds says, "I am glad you were born." If you get this message from a core family member, it adds to your self-worth and self-acceptance, and helps to create a feeling of belonging and importance.

A positive Self-Concept enables us to accept ourselves, in spite of our shortcomings or perceived deficiencies. If we acknowledge ourselves as a work of fine art, a masterpiece constantly evolving, we accept ourselves as we are with the capacity to improve and to become better. Our self-concept is not one, but two-dimensional. Our self-concept is greatly influenced by our thoughts, feelings, and actions. As one of Spirit's creations, we are each in the possession of a Personal Self-Concept Identity and a Spiritual Self-Concept Identity; a Self-Image (inner self-picture) is formed based on the concept we have of ourselves.

Your Identity, used interchangeably with the term Self-Concept, is the core aspect of you. Because of it, there are no two people alike. Spirit created everyone different and unique. Therefore, you are special, one of a kind. Spirit has built within each person a spiritual yardstick to which we should all strive to measure up to. Each lesson is as equally challenging and hard for each person. It is decided before we come to earth the best conditions (parents, race, sex, e.g.) to help us grow and blossom spiritually. The human experience is a refining process necessary for our soul to evolve and develop.

Spirit allows us to decide the particulars of how we want to live our life and what we want to do or accomplish. Some of us decide to come to earth to give joy to our parents for a day, a year, 7 years, or 70 years. Whatever we do with our life, it must be a masterpiece for all to behold. And since no one knows when the final hour will be, it is best that we make each day count. You must do your best daily to be the best person you can be. Sometimes you do not get a second chance to clear up a destructive or unproductive life. It is easy to look at another person and wish you were more like them. Yet, you do not know the pain they endure behind the smile. Remember, you chose this lifetime. You said yes to the Universe and to your life circumstances. The Divine Spirit never promised any of us that we would live a life free of hardship or challenge.

Life is an unpainted canvas. You can create as many scenes as you like. Life is a journey, not a destination. When you stop growing you slowly die, so pause if you must. Take time to enjoy the scenery and the stage production you created. When you die and leave the planet, will your life and living be a masterpiece, or will you give back the heap of ashes from which you came? Who you are is beautiful and magnificent. You are one of a kind, a rare gem.

Your Self-Concept is the basic foundation of who you are. To be fully the person the Divine intended you to be, it will require that you develop both your Personal and Spiritual Self-Concept. Most of us spend little time developing our Spiritual Self-Concept. It is just as important as your Personal Self-Concept. Both aspects of your nature need to be cultivated and built up. Our other basic human needs are support, desire, and self-esteem.

Support – Our Mental, Physical, Emotional Body - We achieve maturity and grow spiritually by working on our mental, physical, and emotional bodies. We have an inner drive to achieve, excel, and be a better person to gain mastery over our lower nature to become the Christ within. We have been given a physical body to work through our imperfections, our negative emotions, and our thoughts of self-doubt. Your goal is to seek ways to improve these three aspects of yourself. This provides the self-discipline you need to complete your primary goal of soul perfection.

Desire – A Dream or a Goal - Believe in yourself, and know you are valuable to life. Like yourself enough to have goals. Be willing to take risks, or plan how you will live your life. The ability to dream or envision a goal is Spirit's divine plan to inspire us to reach and stretch beyond our human limitations. Most big goals, and some little goals, require us to partner with Spirit for their completion and success. Dreams are the longings placed inside of us to help maintain our connection to "It." These are the attributes of a spiritually and whole person: Love/ Unconditional Acceptance, Empathy, Peace, Harmony, Joy, Kindness, Compassion, Tranquility, Gentleness, Consolation, Understanding, Excellence, and Creativity.

Self-Esteem – Our self-concept has many parts; our self-esteem is composed of many selves. Your self-esteem is determined by your cultural upbringing, your morals, and the values of your individual and

14

cultural identities. Your self-esteem tells others how you think and feel about yourself and your relationships with others. Webster's dictionary defines it as "A confidence and satisfaction in oneself." The California State Task Force on Self-Esteem defines it as "Appreciating my own worth, and importance, and having the character to be accountable for myself and to act responsibly towards others."

The way you act is a measure of your self-esteem. You can find more detailed information on this topic in my book *Self-Esteem the Essence of You* at www.idagreene.com

Clear Up Old Baggage From Your Past

It takes courage to clear up the old baggage from our past. Sometimes it may feel easier to cram the feelings of the past down deep into the pit of our soul where it remains stuck as we trod along. Granted there are some things that you might want to set aside to deal with later, but at some point the emotional bill will come due. Eventually all those past hurts, resentments, and frustrations will find a way to burble up and generally at the most inopportune moments, and most definitely during the course of your romantic relationships.

Try this test: Consider how you feel when thinking about the potential of dating and meeting someone new. If your gut reaction is nausea, panic, stress, and basically to run the other way, it is likely have some baggage to sort through. The first step is to simply take inventory. Remember it's taken a long time to gather that baggage, so don't expect to find, clear, and move on from it in a day. It's not really possible to be baggage free, and some baggage can even be helpful—some protects us while we heal—but if you continuously operate on flawed criteria to look for love, it's going to make the search that much more challenging. Commit to tackling your baggage if only one small piece at a time.

Some of these tips may seem overwhelming and big. When I feel like something is too much to tackle I like to remember one of my favorite quotes:

"Inch by inch anything's a cinch."
~ Robert Schuller

Remember, it has taken you a long time; it may seem like a lifetime to collect your emotional baggage, hurts, and habits. Be kind to yourself and be patient in the process of clearing the clutter and energy so you can allow a loving relationship to take the place of what you've cleared away. In doing so, you are making room in your heart, mind, and life to clear the way for love to show up again.

Reclaiming Your Power to Heal Your Inner Pain

We have all been wounded or hurt by someone. To be healed of your emotional wounds, you will need to let go of the stories in your head about who hurt you, when they hurt you, and how they hurt you. Become free from being a victim by choosing to be become detached from your recalled memory of past hurts and wounds. There will always be people who abuse or hurt us unintentionally by living their life as best they know how and being who they are.

Just because we are wounded does not mean we have to take on the role, play the role, or live out our life existence through the role of a victim, or become the "walking wounded". We often take things, people, and the situations that happen to us far too personally. Remember to not take everything that has happened to you in your life "personally".

Things happen and some things are just the way they are. There are billions of people on the planet like you, who are trying to figure why they are here and what they are supposed to do with this thing we have been given called LIFE. Your life is the Inner Power that has been given to you by Divine Spirit to show up and play a bigger game as a player of Greatness in the Game of Life. Your Greatness is your Inner Power to Be, to Do, and to Have. It is time for you to reclaim your

16

Power and live from Your Greatness. It is time to break through to your Greatness.

How to Break Through to Your Best Self

Write down everything that you're afraid of.
1.
2.
3.
4.
5.
6.
7.

How do you want to show up in the world? Do you have a belief about creating value for yourself?

What is it?

What can you do today to create value for yourself?

How can you create value for others through the way you live your life?

Our value in life is created by who we are as well as what we do. Others are watching us to see what use we make of our gifts, talents, and influence, because it determines our greatness.

Both women and men have low self-esteem issues. The uncertainty girls and women have about who they are, and if they are pretty, and if they are as pretty as their peers, and do they fit into the group, or will they find a guy to like or love them—and the comparison list goes on and on? It is no different with men; over 70% of men struggle to express their feelings, which trigger women to feel unsafe around them. Men often view sharing emotions as a sign of weakness.

Men get close through competition and taking action. Women get and feel close in a relationship through talking and sharing. Women want to be in love through connections with men, and to feel that they are important. Men fail at love because they don't treat it as a serious responsibility. Men tie this to their self-worth and feel they are not good as a man. Men lack emotional intelligence and situational awareness. Men don't feel safe to express their true feelings.

Men rarely reach out to support networks, therapists, or a life coach; instead they rely only on themselves. Both women and men press the self-sabotage button without even knowing it. Our ultimate goal is to live from our greatness.

What is Greatness?

Greatness is a mindset of excellence. You have an Inner Power that makes you calm, serene, and peaceful. You have feelings and an attitude of abundance and prosperity. You are able to manifest anything you desire in an instant. Everything you engage in is about Excellence. There is no discord or confusion in your life. What could keep you anchored is your "inner state of knowing" who you are and what you know for certain you can do.

What is Smallness?

Smallness is a state of contraction. The Strength and Source of your Power is on the outside. When you are consumed and controlled by the daily activities that happen to you, you expect the worst outcome because you usually have more bad things than good things happen to you. Your relationships are in disarray, negative, unfulfilling, empty, unrewarding, unloving, petty, vengeful, controlling, conflicting, and constricting.

When your gains in life outweigh your pains, you are on the road to know and experience your Greater Self. Focus your energy by living your vision. Start living now as if everything you desire in life is already in your life, including the right person. Get into the feeling nature of being the best you that you can be. Find out what matters to you and do something about it. When you are attractive, you do not have to wait; you create and draw to you what you desire. Just make sure that when the right person shows up, you have something to share with him or her. These are just some of the things to consider that will help you decide if you have effectively moved through your lost love or if it is still affecting your self-esteem.

Chapter 2
Looking For Love in All the Wrong Places

Do you feel there is something missing in your life? Do you feel incomplete and wish you had someone special to be with? Do you wish you had that special someone in your life who could understand what you feel and how you feel about things that upset you or make you feel sad? Are you tired of being alone and by yourself? Are you attracted to emotionally needy people who demand so much of your attention that you lose sight of yourself? Do you repeatedly become involved with emotionally unavailable people who shut you out no matter what you do? Do you find yourself linked to someone who is emotionally distant, and you feel inadequate as a result? Are you are a rescuer, someone who thinks they can save someone, change someone, or help people in a special way? Love is many things to many people, and it does not mean the same thing to everyone.

It is true that we are made for relationships, and that a relationship can give us a sense of security, comfort, and companionship. Relationships are a lot like an onion—when we peel back the layers of people we discover that all human beings experience emotional pain, hurt, feelings of not being loved, tragedy, emotional abuse, selfishness, selflessness, hurtful words, betrayal, loss, grief, rejection, lost love, lack of caring, indifference, and feelings of abandonment. We tend to look for love in many places; some places and situations work for us, and others lead us to have feelings of frustration, confusion, and feelings of apathy and emptiness.

Looking for Love in the Family

When Love is Not Love

Sex abuse and incest are dirty little secrets in many families. They occur and remain a scourge, because many people confuse sex with love. Sex was designed to help us procreate and multiply the human species. It is a pleasurable act, and many children explore their body parts. It becomes a problem when they explore the body parts of the opposite sex and mating occurs. In many families boys secretly have sex with their sisters, fathers have sex with their daughters, and other males in the family—grandfathers, uncles, and cousins—take advantage of a young child and tell them they love them because they want to have sexual intercourse with them. Little children are not able to know the difference between good touching and bad touching. Touching and stroking the body feels good, and many people confuse sex with love. Sexual intercourse is an adult activity that was intended by the Divine Source of the universe to help us replenish human beings. It was never intended for a man to have sexual intercourse with or impregnate his daughter or the young female in their family or who lives with them. That is sex, and sex has nothing to do with love.

When someone loves you, they do not require you to give them anything in return for their love of you. You are loved for being a Divine being on the planet. You do not need to do anything or be anyone to be genuinely loved. When young girls are sexually abused as children, they live with shame and anger for the rest of their lives. They are often too embarrassed to say anything to anyone, because they feel unclean, dirty, and unworthy of being loved for who they are. They feel traumatized and violated, and it leaves a hole in their souls that lasts for a lifetime. It often causes many women to feel uncomfortable being naked in the presence of a mature male/female relationship and feeling frigid in a male/female sex encounter. Sexual abuse of a child is wrong whether it is a man having sex with a boy, a woman having sex with a boy, or a man having sexual intercourse with a girl. This has become a silent spiritual plague in our society that is worse than any leprosy could have ever been in the history of mankind. We have lost our purpose and our Divine reason to love and be loved.

These Are Some of the Places We Look for Love:

21

Looking for Love in Bars/Night Clubs

Although, it is fun to dance, drink liquor, and socialize, this is not the best situation to find someone who is rational and remembers what they said or what commitment they may have while in a false state of euphoria. I took my cousin out to a night club to help her find a boyfriend, and I left the club with one. I had not planned on talking to anyone. This guy asked me to dance, and I could not get away from him. He ended up taking me home along with his friend, who I found out later was his date for that night. The next day when I left church, he was parked outside in his car waiting for me. Then he was waiting for me when I got home from work every night at 1 am. We talked until 5 am in the morning, and then he went home. He worked out of town driving trucks, and we missed each other a lot. We eventually got married. The marriage did not last long and did not turn out well. This was my first introduction to domestic violence.

We Look for Love on Social Media

Although some people find their life partner on E-Harmony, Craigslist, Facebook, texting sexting, and other dating services, there are many people who are jilted, misled, and taken advantage of through social media. I joined E-Harmony and met a nice guy. I had always wanted to meet a man with good computer skills since that is an area where I am weak. He helped me with a lot of my computer challenges. He was divorced from his wife; his daughter whom he loved dearly lived with her mom and he lived alone. I went to his house to spend Labor Day with him. He went to the store to buy the food for our dinner. I cooked the main course and he cooked the dessert. I enjoyed spending the day with him. I do not spend the night at men's houses, so I left his house at 3 am, because we had a wonderful conversation with him showing me all his art and telling about all the things he had done. He went to several events with me in San Diego where I was a speaker and doing clairaudient readings. He drove up to Los Angeles to attend a workshop that I put together with a male friend on "How Finding a Good Man". I really enjoyed his company, however he was part of a sect that traveled around the country with a Master Guru from India. I am my own guru. I am a follower of Jesus, and he gives me the freedom to do what I want, when I want, and to do as I please. I respect that he had a calling to do what he was doing. He left San Diego all dressed in white with his group and I never saw him again. I loved and enjoyed the times we spent together and when we went out to eat; he was a strict vegetarian. I enjoyed his showing me how to stand and balance myself on one foot and how to do Sufi dancing.

We Look for Love in the Churches, Synagogues, and Spiritual Centers

This can be a safe environment because you can check out the person's references through the church grapevine. Plus you will definitely learn about the good, bad, and ugly if the priest, rabbi, or minister marries you.

We Look for Love as a Wife, Mom, Husband, or Father

I was married two times, and I did not feel loved by either of my husbands. I thought by being a wife I would find love or be loved. I wanted to have children, but my body aborted the pregnancy two times with my first husband. I am thankful that I did not get pregnant by my second husband who had me do a lot of fertility testing because he wanted me to have his child. He was an Alcoholic; Bipolar and physically abusive. I did not want a child to endure the abuse I was enduring with him. My desire to not be alone and to have a family allowed me to marry my first husband who died of pneumonia at an early age. Sexual attraction brought me together with my second husband, but it was not enough to sustain the relationship. Plus my husband a problem with women, and had relationships with several women in the presence of my foster son, who we were parenting. When I complained about his marital affairs and decided to divorce him, his physical abuse of me began on a regular basis. I ended the marriage because I did not want to go to prison. I could not handle his physical beatings of me and was thinking of ways I could kill him. After much consultation with my attorney, I entered a shelter, filed a restraining order on him, and left with my foster son to live with a coworker temporarily.

Unusual Places We May Find Love:

Airplanes/Other Forms of Travel

I did have one lady tell me that she found love on an airplane, so you never know who that special someone may be sitting next to you on the airplane. So look and smell your best the next time you travel by air, on a bus, coaster train, or on a ship because I did find love on a cruise.

Networking Events

Networking is an ideal place to meet new people for your business, friendships, acquaintances, or romantic adventure.

Grocery Stores/Shopping/Car Dealership

You never know who or what you may find when you are out shopping beside groceries, so dress and smell your best when you leave home. I went shopping for a car one time and met a man who was attracted to me. We dated for about six months, and while I was out of town, I found out that he had a lady's phone number in his wallet. I checked out the address thinking I would find him there and found his wife. They were separated and living in different houses. I do not date married men, so I told him I would have to stop seeing him. He came back by my house 10 years later and had divorced his wife however I had moved on and was no longer interested in him.

What is Love and How Do You Get It or Find It?

I say love is a "many splendid thing". It comes in many forms, languages, cultures, shapes, sizes, skin tones, beliefs, religions, relationships, emotions, feelings, work settings, family settings, sport settings, and in the mind and hearts of an individual. Love is everywhere, yet most of us feel unloved, unwanted, not cared about, needed, or appreciated. If love is everywhere as I suspect it is; why do you think we are unable to see it, feel it, or detect its presence in our lives? Have you ever wondered about that? I have and sometimes I have to do a self-inventory to see if I am loved and to remind myself that I am loved. In addition, in many of our families, we do not verbally express our love or caring for each other, because we do not have the language or proper way to say what we want to share. In many cases it is assumed that our family members know we love them, and this could not be further from the truth. We are often not shown how to say or how to show that we care. It is much easier to share our negative thoughts than it is to share our positive thoughts and feelings.

The main way we show love is through our nonverbal and verbal communication. Although we are verbal communicators, we are nonverbal when it comes to love. We are not good verbal communicators when it comes to love. Partly because love is a heart-feeling connection that is not easily understood, so most of us do not know how to express love or show love. We are not taught or trained on how to show our love or our caring, therefore we do not know how to do it, and we often do not recognize love when it shows up in our lives. This is because love has to do with the quality and value of our communication and we are deficient when it comes to communicating what we value, who we value, in what way we value it or them. As a child I felt my mom did not love me; however, as an adult I realized that my mom showed her love for me by focusing on my being more ladylike, because I was constantly climbing, sitting with my legs open, and exposing my underwear. She also showed her love for me by preparing my favorite food for me. My mom gave us all love through food.

It can be difficult to explain why we feel a certain way about someone if we or they have not taken the time to communicate with us or share how they feel about us. It is awkward; and we do not know how to share platonic love or how to communicate it. Men tend to show their love in a factual manner, without feelings, and women tend to show their love through doing something for the person in a nurturing or caretaking manner.

The media shows and tell us how to communicate erotic love or love making in an intimate setting; however, no one tells or shows us how to show genuine feelings of caring or platonic feelings of love. Have you ever wondered what it would be like to communicate quality and values in your relationship with others?

How to Communicate Quality and Values

Your values determine what's really most important in your life. So, what is most important in your life right now? Your values are the underlying foundational pieces that you've determined to be the most important parts of your life. In other words, it's those standards and principles that you truly stand for. It's what you fight for and take a stand for. It's what you would be willing to risk embarrassment for. It's what you would be willing to speak out for even if the numbers were not in your favor. And it's what you might even be willing to put your life on the line for. So, what is it that you truly value the most? Is it health? Is it family? Is it freedom? Liberty? Or is it love? What is it that you truly value? Find out and live accordingly.

Your priorities are the day-to-day choices you make about the activities you determine to be most important to you. Typically people's priorities are correlated with their values—maybe not exactly, but there is a significant correlation. Your values system will help you to determine what's most important to do every day. And furthermore, your values and priorities will help keep you on the path of your purpose and your vision, because they should all be in alignment with each other. Let me repeat that: Your values on love, your vision for love, and your purpose for being on the planet should all be in alignment with each other, and if love is not one of your core values, you will have a deficit of love feelings for yourself and others.

26

All people have the unique gift to communicate principles of quality and to share their values. They have the ability to bring people together for a common cause to help them to grow and develop as a team member and work for the common good of a project at hand. Good leaders project charisma, caring feelings, self-confidence, and loving feelings for others. They send a message to others that they can be trusted to take charge of the task at hand to produce a positive outcome, because they care about the feelings and welfare of others. When we do not feel loved, appreciated, or cared about, we will find a way to fill the void or emptiness, and sometimes our need to feel loved will be filled through the use of substances or food. Do you use food to fill a lack of or a void of love? Take the inventory below to find out.

Are You Using Food to Fill the Void of Love?

Are You an Eating Disorder Codependent?

Use this questionnaire from Fat is a Family Affair to evaluate the extent of your involvement with an under or overeater of food. Answer each question below for yourself.

What Works When "Diets" Don't?

Do you force yourself to be on diets?

Do you threaten to leave your partner due to weight?

Do you check on your/the diet constantly?

Do you make promises based on pounds lost or gained?

Do you hide food from an overeater?

Do you worry incessantly about an undereater?

Have you "walked on eggshells" so as not to upset the over/undereater?

Do you throw food away so the overeater won't find it?

Have you excused the erratic, sometimes violent mood swings resulting from sugar binges?

Do you change social activities so the overeater won't be tempted?

Do you manipulate budgets to control spending on food and clothing?

Do you purchase and promote eating the "right" foods?

Do you promote gyms, health spas, and miracle cures?

Do you break into emotional tirades when you catch the overeater bingeing?

Are you constantly disappointed when you see a relapse?

Are you embarrassed by the over/undereater's appearance?

Do you falsely console the over/undereater when he or she is embarrassed?

Have you lowered your expectations of what you might like?

Does your weight fluctuate with your loved one's (you up, he or she down)?

Have you stopped attending to your own grooming?

Do you have many aches and pains and a preoccupation with health?

Are you drinking heavily or using sleeping pills or tranquilizers?

Do you bribe with food?

Do you talk about the eater's body to him or her or to others?

Do you feel life will be perfect if the over/undereater shaped up?

Are you grateful you aren't "that bad"?

Boundaries

Boundaries are the dividing lines that separate you from others, or where you end and other people begin. This includes understanding what your limits are, what your needs are, and what is unacceptable for you. You can quickly see how your deal-makers and your deal-breakers will help you to define some of your boundaries. This includes being proactive or assertive and asking for what you want. On the other hand, it's also letting people know what you don't want or what is unacceptable for you. If you do this you will create your highest self-respect and self-esteem. We need to know, practice, and learn from our boundaries.

Your boundaries are even more than that. You also have boundaries that you set with yourself. What this means is to set boundaries between different parts of your life, so, for example, you don't become a workaholic. Finding time for your friends, time to exercise, and time just to rest and relax would all be examples of you setting boundaries with yourself so you can have the most balance possible in your life.

In this day and age there is a big invitation out there to get into a workaholic mode of "bigger, better, faster, more, now" which seems to be the paradigm many people and businesses operate from. When you have inner boundaries with yourself and have external boundaries, both together makes for a winning combination. Without boundaries you never know what might happen.

How to Create Boundaries Around Things You Love

It is easier to create boundaries around an object than it is to create boundaries around your feelings and matters of the heart. I suggest you first create boundaries around your money so that your heart cannot be manipulated to separate you from your money. It is easier to start protecting your money so that you will have the practice on how to not let others use your emotions to control your heart strings. It is alright to love money for the things it affords you to have, and the things it affords you to do to help others; however, money can never be a replacement for the love your heart and emotions need and want. Your relationships should never suffer because of the time you spend making money. Money is a tool you need and use to provide for yourself and your family. You need the skills of money making and money saving. However, your love making skills of showing affection, tenderness, compassion, empathy, and sympathy can be useful in getting and keeping money.

These are some of the emotional traits that you want to let go of; Fear, Impatience, Frustration, Envy, Jealousy, Criticism, Complaining, Anger, and Rage. Confusion and frustration can quickly arise inside us when we feel we won't ever have enough to meet our needs, goals, or desires. Our ego is a desiring machine that is always wanting, wanting. It does not know what is, true heart satisfaction. It is only through your heart that you will find the feeling of being enough and having enough. When you are enough and have enough emotionally it will manifest into your outer experience of having a sense of well-being which will give you the feeling of I am enough, because I know how to create whatever I need including love. The secret to manifesting love is a lot like manifesting anything else you want in your life.

These are some of the things that get in the way of people finding the right lover or love relationship:

1. Not knowing what you're looking for; having unclear expectations.

30

2. Having a long "grocery list" of what you want in a relationship and looking for the one person to fill it.

3. Living in fear that you will repeat past experiences.

4. Not healing before starting a new relationship.

5. Women fearing that their biological clock is running out.

6. Men having a fear of starting a family and staying committed.

7. Lowering of standards by older singles, giving up or settling, because they are afraid they will always be alone.

8. Not knowing where to meet other singles with whom you might be compatible.

9. Being too busy to date or cultivate a relationship.

10. Discouragement of not finding someone who meets your expectations.

11. Expectations for sex conflicting with how you feel about the person.

12. Cynicism about women or men.

13. Getting involved too quickly.

14. Not knowing how to start a conversation with a date or potential partner.

15. Having a belief mentality that there are "no good men, no good women".

16. Pressure from family or peers to be coupled.

17. Not having the skills to create a successful relationship.

18. Having a fear of failure around your ability to attract a companion.

19. Fear of rejection that no one would, or could like you.

20. Fear of commitment.

21. Shyness.

22. It is easier to stay single rather than go to the trouble of changing to find the love you want.

Look over this list, find the ones that apply to you, then, discuss them with a Relationship Coach like myself. You can call me to get a free 30-minute coaching session to help you refine what you really want in a loving relationship. I can be reached at 619-262-9951 or www.idagreene.com.

Relationships, the Connection of Us and Others

The quality of your life is the direct result of the quality of your relationships—with your divine source, with yourself, and with others. The fastest way to help improve your relationships is to realign your ego with its true nature to serve as a joyful servant of your soul. If you want to break your old patterns of behavior, you will need to retrain your brain to function in harmony with your true nature of peace and then align your actions with your most deeply held values of love and connection with others. When you are you ready, realign your ego to your inner being (soul), and let it serve as a tool to help you connect with others. Follow these guidelines to have a better relationship connection with others.

* Allow your personal compass of love to keep you on track even when you are in the difficult situations. Love has boundaries and is not abuse.

* Learn how to hone your intuitive sense so you trust yourself and others more easily.

* Compromise can wreak havoc in your relationships; learn how to collaborate.

* Learn how to take action from seeking the truth rather than reacting to fear.

* Find how you can experience everyone and everything as a source of love rather than as a source of conflict.

Love is the place you are coming from; it is your being. You are love. Love is the divine force everywhere, the universal energy, the moving power of life that flows in your own heart. Love is accepting someone as they are and not trying to change them to be who you want them to be.

Relationships and Chemistry

Linda Marshall, M.Div., Director of Couples Programs for the Relationship Coaching Institute, says, "Love is not an emotion, but a physiological drive that is as powerful as hunger and that phenyl ethylamine (PEA for short) acts as a love drug that stimulates feelings of euphoria during the early stage of a relationship. She quotes that this altered state of infatuation suppresses the part of our brain which is designed to warn and protect us from danger." This helps to explain our euphoria and why we may act like we under the influence of a drug.

Author, anthropology professor, and human behavior researcher, Helen Fisher, Ph.D., is one of the major researchers in the field of interpersonal chemistry. She has studied romantic love in 170 societies and found it to be a universal phenomenon and bears all the basic characteristics of addiction. In her research, she has found that MRI images of the brain reveal that the cognitive area of our brain actually loses blood when we are in love.

Dr. Fisher's research has revealed that there are different hormones driving sex, romance, and attachment, the three most common aspects of love. Fisher reveals that love is not an emotion but a physiological drive as powerful as hunger. Romantic love is actually a basic drive that has evolved for the purposes of mating and reproduction.

Sex

The sex drive is driven by testosterone, a libido-enhancing, energy producing chemical secreted in the testes of males and ovaries of females. On average, men produce about 20 times more testosterone than women. What do you suppose that means for the attraction factor for women? It may explain why some women are slow to take action in starting a romantic encounter.

Romance

In the breathless phase of romantic attraction we are elated, full, and overflowing with energy and obsessed with our love interest, thinking of them almost every waking second and often dreaming of them while we sleep. This is a period of extreme pleasure in which we feel more alive and are more alert, thinking and acting more quickly than usual.

This response is involuntary and enhanced by increased levels of naturally-occurring dopamine and norepinephrine. Novelty of any kind, especially when infatuated in a new relationship, increases levels of these two chemicals in our brains. The elevated activity of these two "love drugs" increases the production of testosterone, linking our attraction to someone with our desire for them sexually. It is a time when sexual tension is overpowering. An interesting phenomenon that occurs simultaneously is a decrease in serotonin, the chemical that eases tension and produces a sensation of relaxation. Our system is truly excited and experiencing a sustained "high".

During this time we focus our attention on our love interest, and everything that occurs between us takes on special meaning. Along with our euphoria commonly comes swings of insecurity and fear that our love interest isn't as interested as we. We develop an emotional dependence upon the other and experience separation anxiety when not in their presence. Our craving for emotional union is intense and difficult to control. We can become possessive as we guard our lover from the intrusion of any outside threat. We are protecting life's greatest prize—a mating partner.

Fisher states that in general, men are more visually stimulated because their brains are wired to accommodate their search for a woman to give them healthy babies, while the memory part of a woman's brain is wired to accommodate her need to find a man who keeps his promises. And thus this ensures the survival of our species.

Attachment

Love changes over time. Eventually the euphoria subsides as we settle into the next phase, attachment, characterized by feelings of security and calm. At this point, oxytocin and vasopressin are the chemicals at play in our bodies. Oxytocin is released during orgasm in both the male and the female. In the brain, both these chemicals are involved in social behavior and bonding. Researchers believe these chemicals are in play in supporting the formation of trust between two people and the bond they experience during sexual activity.

The Four Basic Personality Types

Dr. Fisher is the guiding force behind the matching technology of the online dating service, Chemistry.com. It has long been known that we tend to be attracted to people similar to ourselves—with the same ethnic, social, religious, educational, and economic background. This also extends to our attraction to people with a similar amount of physical attractiveness, a comparable intelligence, and parallel attitudes, expectations, values, and interests. What is only beginning to be known is that the chemicals in our bodies affect our personalities. Dr. Fisher has identified four personality styles that accompany the characteristic dominant level of one of four hormones: dopamine, serotonin, estrogen, and testosterone. These personality styles are also predictive of whom we are more likely to be attracted.

Higher Dopamine = "Explorer"

Someone with high levels of dopamine Fisher calls an "Explorer". What makes an explorer a desirable partner is their high energy, high creativity, and spontaneity. They tend to be artistic and seek novelty, risk, and pleasure. They are intellectually curious and not easily swayed by the opinions of others. The challenges in relating to an explorer are their propensity toward addiction and their tendency to philander.

Higher Serotonin = "Builder"

Someone with high levels of serotonin Fisher calls a "Builder". What makes a builder a desirable partner is their calm demeanor and low anxiety. They have a deep attachment to their home and family and are often consistent, loyal, and protective of those they love. They have managerial skills, are sympathetic, and cooperative. They work hard and have a lot of common sense. Their patience gives them the ability to complete detailed, painstaking jobs more easily than most people. The challenge in relating to a builder is their propensity to be "right" and to know the "right way" to do things.

Higher Estrogen = "Negotiator"

Someone with high levels of estrogen Fisher calls a "Negotiator". What makes a negotiator a desirable partner is their idealistic, big picture thinking. They are relational, egalitarian, non-hierarchical, intuitive, flexible, and excel at long-term planning and consensus building. They usually have high verbal and social skills, tending to be networkers who are imaginative, capable of deep empathy, and nurturing. The challenge in relating to a negotiator is their absolute need to establish a deep connection with you.

Higher Testosterone = "Director"

Someone with high levels of testosterone she calls a "Director". What makes a director a desirable partner is their daring, originality, directness, and inventiveness. They usually are good leaders who are conscious of rank and appropriate behavior. Achieving positions of power and influence often comes easily to them. They can be very assertive and tough minded, focusing on schedules, rules, and routines. They tend to be competitive and efficient. As an independent thinker, they are skilled at abstract thinking and short-term planning. The challenge in relating to a director is their mental inflexibility and limited social sensitivity.

According to Dr. Fisher, Builders are best matched with Explorers, and Directors are best matched with Negotiators. Negotiators, with their flexibility, empathy, and nurturing abilities, are compatible and sought after by all the other personality styles. There is little published information about these personality types at this time.

Conscious Mating

Conscious Mating requires that we understand what motivates us, what we are feeling, and why we are feeling it. We are complex creatures driven by primal biological forces as well as our higher cognitive abilities. All successful relationships depend upon our ability to make good long-term partner choices; and understanding the chemistry of love enables us to balance our heart with our head.

The Journey to Find Love or Be Loved

As you continue on your journey to find the lover of your life, there are other things you want to keep in mind. Clean up your living space. It is hard to attract a new love or lover into your life when there is a lot of clutter in your mind or your life. This may sound weird, but cleaning up your living space will help you in your pursuit of love. Consider looking at your physical space from the perspective of someone seeing it for the first time. What does your living space say about you? Does it feel inviting? Warm? Cozy? Or does it feel more like a bachelor/ette crash pad where you store your dirty laundry?

Ask a friend for their opinion on this. Your living space is an outward reflection of your inner life. Consider what your living space says to others who are on the outside looking in? I find that when I straighten up my living space and clear out my clutter, I'm better able to focus more on the important things, like nurturing a love interest or getting excited about the idea of meeting new people or finding a new lover or love.

I just got rid of some old books and papers of 10 years ago, and I was surprised how energized I felt getting rid of my clutter. There were some old feelings and emotions that I had to let go of to move on, and to accept that I did the best I could under the circumstances with the information and knowledge I had at the time. I am more emotionally mature now, so I do not take things as personally. Neither do I feel mortally wounded by what has happened to me like I used to feel. Life has a way of forcing us to live with the pain and agony of our past or to turn the page of our life to a new chapter in our relationships to see the possibility of a new lover or a new platonic friendship or relationship. There are many traps in dating to find a new love relationship.
Use the following checklist to identify possible red flags in a prospective relationship you may be considering.

Conscious Dating Red Flags

Your Name   Potential Partner

Date   **Y or N**

1. Would I want to spend the rest of my life with this person exactly as they are?

2. Would I want this person to raise my child?

3. Would I want my child to be exactly like this person?

4. Do I want to rescue or "help" them because I see their potential?

5. I love the way they look or their status, and it builds my self-esteem to be with them.

6. We have some things in common and so I'm avoiding looking at glaring differences.

7. They appear to be totally different than people I've been with in the past.

8. I'm focusing on one important quality (money, sex, fun, humor, etc.) and ignoring unmet requirements.

9. Reacts to frustration with anger, rage, blame.

10. Blames others or circumstances for life situation.

11. Tries to control everything, including me.

12. Immature, impulsive, and/or irresponsible.

13. Emotionally distant or void, aloof.

14. Still pining for a past relationship.

15. Someone who wants me to make their sad life better.

16. Married or otherwise unavailable to commit to me.

17. Active addiction, addictive behavior (rationalized as "not a problem").

18. Is pessimistic and negative about things that matter to the man.

19. Lacks integrity in dealing with people, money, etc.

20. Judgmental attitude toward themselves and others.

21. Unwilling to self-examine, accept feedback, take responsibility.

22. Doesn't keep agreements.

23. What she/he says about him/herself doesn't match reality.

24. Emotional roller coaster, recurring, or regular emotional drama.

25. This isn't what I really want, but I don't want to be alone.

26. Changeable, inconsistent behavior.

27. Inability to listen.

28. I notice myself trying to change this person to fit what I want, instead of accepting them for who they are.

29. Talks too much (especially about self), monopolizes conversation.

30. Overly quiet, withdrawn.

Total the checked items. Circle the ones that need close attention, decision-making, or require more information.

On a scale from 0 (Not at all) to 100 (Perfect fit) my minimum score for considering any relationship is _____
Using the above scale I score this potential relationship _____.
Based upon the above results, I should proceed dating this potential partner. Y   N
I should not proceed dating this potential partner. Y   N

If it's clear you should not proceed dating this potential partner and you have any difficulty moving on, show this checklist to your best friend, close family member, therapist, or coach and get the support you need.

The Secret to Manifesting Love

The secret to manifesting enough love is to soak and rest in the feeling of love throughout your day that "**you**" are enough. When you realize this, everything changes. You naturally start creating abundant feelings about your love situation which is supported by your positive empowering beliefs about love. The truth is that no matter how much love you have, your ego will never ever feel that it is enough. We will never feel that we are adequate. We all have feelings of self-doubt about whether we are pretty enough, tall enough, have the right body size, hips, breast, or bra size, right lip thickness or curve, right dress size, the skin tone or color, the right hair length, color, or thickness. We are obsessed with the question: Am I enough to attract the man/woman of my dreams? It is only when you meditate on and connect with your spiritual inner self that you will be able to see the beauty inside you, and when you see your inner beauty everyone will see it as well.

Your feelings of love deprivation and your feelings of being alone and without love will loom big in your life as long as you see this as a problem. Anything that we focus on will become bigger in our life, be it lack of love, lack of attention, being overly shy, or not knowing how to make friends. It will all become a bigger problem, the more we see it a problem without a solution. We must give others the freedom to like us or to not like us, to love us or to not love us. Do not become attached to or resist being liked or loved by someone else. People will either like you or not like you. They will either love you or not love you, and you have no control over it. Strive to like yourself and become a likable or loving human being who deserves to be loved for being who you are. Learn to be at peace with yourself with or without a man/woman or having someone love you.

When you start thinking, feeling, and vibrating like a lover, you will become more attractive to others. The key is to be in a constant state of acceptance and gratitude for who you are. See and know that you are the essence of love at the core of your being. Being with this feeling and knowing is a spiritual awakening experience. Sit in the core of the feeling of love on a daily basis. Take a step back and observe any judgments that arise inside you without getting entangled in your story about how love should look or how love should show up in your life. Just be with the feeling of the absence of love until it passes or until you feel comfortable in letting it be or allowing yourself to not have love or be loved every second of the day. Eventually the tension you feel and your fears around Love will fade away and you will feel a release inside you that lifts you to a higher vibration, and a lighter feeling of love will begin to expand inside you.

AFTER A WHILE

Veronica Shoftshall

After a while you learn the subtle difference
between holding a hand and chaining a soul
and you learn that love doesn't mean leaning
and company doesn't always mean security.

And you begin to learn that kisses aren't contracts
and presents aren't promises
and you begin to accept your defeats with your head up
and your eyes open with the grace of an adult,
not the grief of a child

And you learn to build all your roads on today
because tomorrow's ground is too uncertain for plans
and futures have a way of falling down in mid-flight.

After a while you learn that even sunshine burns
if you get too much
so you plant your own garden and decorate your own soul instead of
waiting for someone to bring you flowers.

And you learn that you really can endure
you really are strong you really do have worth.

I Love Myself the Way I Am

Jai Michael Josephs

I love myself the way I am, there's nothing I need to change.

I'll always be the perfect me; there's nothing to rearrange.

I'm beautiful and capable of being the best me I can.

And, I love myself just the way I am.

I love you the way you are; there's nothing you need to do.

When I feel the love inside myself, it's easy to love you.

Behind your fears, your rage and tears, I see your shining star.

And, I love you just the way you are.

I love the world the way it is, 'cause I can clearly see

That all the things I judge are done by people just like me.

So 'til the birth of peace on earth that only love can bring,

I'll help it grow by loving everything.

I love myself just the way I am and still I want to grow.

But change outside can only come when deep inside I know

I'm beautiful and capable of being the best me I can.

And, I love myself just the way I am.

I love myself just the way I am.

Chapter 3
How to Find the Right Loving Relationship

Here are some suggestions from Relationship Coach, Rori Raye, who says her biggest credential is that she has been blissfully married for 20 years. She says it has not always been that way. According to her, she says: "I used to use all the wrong words and actions to attract and keep a man in my life. In fact, I almost lost my husband completely until I learned to say right things and behave in the right way."

According to her, she says, "My relationship changed practically overnight when I learned that in order to inspire his total devotion, I needed to stop using all the wrong ways that most women think work to get love, but really just push men away. These ways prevent men from connecting with you—deeply and emotionally—so your relationships are only temporary or will never happen at all. All they ever lead to are a buddy, a 'player' or a man just 'passing through' on his way to the 'real' love of his life. And you need to stop taking them for granted if you want to inspire his affection and commitment."

These are some of the ways she says that work and do not work.

Wrong Way #1: **The Logical MIND**
You can shine during a discussion and you have a lot in common. You'll impress a man and make him enjoy your company, but you may feel disappointed to learn that he feels no CHEMISTRY with you. That's because when you try to connect with a man through his mind,

he doesn't FEEL anything. Oh, he may "enjoy being with you", but he just never gets TOUCHED by you in a deep, connected, emotional sense. He never feels like he's about to lose control of himself and fall in love.

Wrong Way #2: **The Physical Road (BODY)**
Despite what a lot of women think, men do not become attached through sex, even if it's fabulous. We've all been sold on the idea that a woman who likes sex and is "good" in bed is ALL IMPORTANT to a man. And it's not. It's just a small part of the whole picture for him. All it **does** is give you is a "sex buddy". Not a partner, not a boyfriend, not a husband. You'll also end up with a broken heart because you'll get attached and he won't want anything "real" with you.

Wrong Way #3: **The Spiritual Road** (SPIRIT)
I meet many women who value their spiritual beliefs and want to be with a man who **shares** their values and spiritual interest and commitment. And it's so easy to mistake the friendship that can grow between two people who worship in the same way, who care about the same things, for a passionate, emotional bond. And yet, all that will get you—at best—is a deep friendship. He'll tell everyone what a great woman you are, but he won't be dreaming about you night after night or longing to hold you in his arms.

The Right Way to Inspire a Man's Devotion: In order to connect with a man's heart so he'll feel compelled to be with you and worship and adore you the way you deserve, you have to drop down into YOUR heart first. Once he feels your heart, he'll open up his, creating a heart-to-heart connection that begins with expressing your feelings and being your most feminine, authentic self. Most women buy into the lie that "men don't like emotions". But the truth is, a man LOVES to share his emotions. He yearns for a woman who can help him feel his own feelings and therefore allow him to be himself. If you're not in touch with your feelings, he won't feel safe expressing his.

The trick is to learn exactly "how" to express your feelings—in words that will draw a man closer in an amazing way. The usual way we express our feelings comes out sounding either, stifled, inauthentic, or critical to a man and does nothing to connect with his heart. You must learn how to express your feelings and really connect with a man and inspire his love. Your "body language" must be sensuous so that it magnetizes his attention and so you do not seem to be chasing him or acting fake.

Thoughts to Ponder

• Independence of thoughts and action is strength of character.

• Compassion means to release all judgment about yourself and others; focus on the love, light, and good that is within everyone including you.

• Love you, others, and every situation no matter what the outward appearance may be.

• Integrity is doing the right thing.

• To increase your self-esteem, stand up for what you believe is right.

• A person with high self-esteem believes in themselves, their ability to provide and take care of themselves, and they do not rely on others to provide or take care of them.

• A person with high self-esteem knows that they are worthy of Spirit's love for them regardless of what they may have done; they are given another chance to correct their faults and shortcomings.

• A person with high self-esteem works to be independent of the thoughts, feelings, attitudes, and negative beliefs others may hold about them.

• Compassion is to have sympathy and empathy for the feelings and predicaments of others.

• To love is to open your heart to the faults, shortcomings, and mistake of others and to do the same for yourself and to suspend your judgments.

• Commitment allows you to let go of your fears of what could happen. It allows you to stay around long enough to see what happens and work through the rough spots to get to the other side of the situation or matter of concern.

• Love means never having to say you are sorry.

• You know others love you by the way they respect you, take care of your feelings, and are willing to put forth the effort to correct any perceptions of lack of love or any intention to hurt you.

• People who love you watch what they say and do to you and avoid doing or saying things they feel might, hurt, offend, or demean you or your character.

• Takers care only about what is best for them.

A Fine Line Separates Love and Abuse

Abuse is about Power and Control, and abuse is very common. The abuser feels alone and only has value when he is in control of another person. As we all know, abused people will enter into an abusive relationship, or they will be self-abusive. And maybe you can elaborate on some of that because that was a very important part how we started working on these concepts.

You are "no good"! The abused person loves to hear those words, because they are convinced that they're defective because the abuser tells them they're defective. As a child with infantile feelings of omnipotence, they blame themselves for what happened in their family life. They take the rap, and the whole story or theme is reinforced and carried throughout their life into adulthood with the same habit patterns being played out as an adult.

I am learning that similar is not equal and not to abuse myself. What happened was my father would say the words to me, "That is stupid" and I took that to mean I was stupid. So I had a subconscious belief that I was stupid even though I never spoke about this to anyone. These thoughts were playing back to me. And then I learned we can abuse ourselves through the thoughts we think continuously.

When I felt suicidal, I thought that there was no hope. That everything in my life would stay the same until I discussed it with a relationship coach and realized that I had the power to change the circumstances in my life.

How to Cope with Verbally Abusive People

Verbal abuse is not something you should tolerate any time, any place or with anyone. But in order to combat it, you need to figure out what is the best approach for you to take. "People who are verbally abusive put people on the defensive," says Patricia Evans, an interpersonal communications expert and author of *The Verbally Abusive Relationship: How to Recognize it and How to Respond* (Adams Media Corporation). She recommends, rather than trying to defend yourself, respond with to the verbal abuser with, "What did you say?" or "Let me write that down."

Also, document your abuser's outbursts and ask the abuser to provide a record of everything you're asked to do to avoid being blamed for his or her mistakes. Before taking drastic measures, talk to the abuser—when he or she is calm—about how you can both communicate more effectively.

Although being the target of verbal abuse can make you want to throw in the towel, it can also become an opportunity for change. For example, in my book *Anger Management Skills for Women and for Men*, I offer an assessment that helps you identify that you're the cause of the anger and I suggest ways in which you can learn to work with conflicting personality types.

Although dealing with verbal abuse is a sensitive issue, being targeted may give you the impetus to release the personal baggage that is preventing you from reaching your potential.

What if You Are the Abuser?

Do your subordinates or co-workers dip into their offices when they see you stomping down the hall? If you're the office meaner, it's time to turn your behavior around. "If you want to know if you're a verbally abusive boss or co-worker", says Arthur Bell, "look for symptoms." According to Bell, this involves "managing by anger, not by encouragement." Impacting others in a way that produces silence, sullenness, and hurt feelings may be a sign.

To change your behavior, take the time to learn more about why you feel the need to strike out. "Verbal abuse is about a loss of power," says Ruth King, the author of *Healing Rage: Women Making Inner Peace Possible.* "It's about shame, fear, and feeling highly controlled and out of control. Usually people in these situations were victims and have now become perpetrators," she says.

Most importantly, learn to take a time out. King suggests implementing a stillness practice for five minutes every morning. Notice your thoughts, and take the time to set an intention for your day. Learn to know what love is and what love is not.

Shakespeare Quotations on Love

My bounty is as boundless as the sea,
My love as deep; the more I give to thee,
The more I have, for both are infinite.
(*Romeo and Juliet*, 2.2.139-41)

Hear my soul speak: The very instant that I saw you, did
My heart fly to your service.
(*The Tempest*, 3.1.60-3)

Who ever loved that loved not at first sight?
(*As You Like It*, 3.5.84)

This bud of love, by summer's ripening breath,
May prove a beauteous flower when next we meet.
(*Romeo and Juliet*, 2.2.121-2)

Love looks not with the eyes, but with the mind,
And therefore is winged Cupid painted blind.
(*A Midsummer Night's Dream*, 1.1.231-2)

If thou remembers not the slightest folly
That ever love did make thee run into,
Thou hast not loved.
(*As You Like It*, 2.4.33-5)

Eternity was in our lips and eyes,
Bliss in our brows' bent; none our parts so poor
But was a race of heaven.
(*Antony and Cleopatra*, 1.3.36-8)

Doubt thou the stars are fire;
Doubt that the sun doth move;
Doubt truth to be a liar; But never doubt I love.

(*Hamlet*, 1.2.123-6)

On Self-Acceptance

Some of these are quotes used by Maxie C. Maultsby Jr., M.D., at the Rational Behavior Therapy Center. "I am a person with human dignity. What I do does not change me. Sometimes I make mistakes, and sometimes I do things very well, but I am the same person no matter what I do.

I will continue to make some mistakes throughout my life because I'm not perfect: I am a fallible human being. However, because I am a person, I also have the ability to learn. I can work on mistakes and learn to do what is necessary to change them. I can strive to "do" better; I cannot "be" better. I already am a human being.

The past is in the past. I cannot change that. I regret some things I've done. I don't like some things that have happened, but I cannot change the past by staying upset and worried. I can't guarantee the future by being worried either.

I can change my feelings right now. I am probably going to handle situations better if I'm calmer and more clearheaded.

I am remembering that I am in control of my feelings. I control myself. I can't always control the situation.

Many times things happen that I don't like. I will accept this by remembering that I cannot control everything.

If I don't like it, I can do my best to do something about it, if I want to. If I don't want to, I can calmly remember that I have a choice.

Other people control their decisions about their behavior. You are not responsible for what other people think, feel, or do.

I want to do my best to help others, but their behavior is in their control. They decide what they do.

I do what I do because I can only act in light of my own experience, my own learning, and my own attitudes.

Sometimes I make mistakes; this doesn't mean I'm bad or wrong. A mistake means I don't know everything.

No one knows everything. I am a human being who has the ability to learn from my mistakes.

What people think or do cannot make you less of a person. You are you and no one can change you.

I will continue to do things I do and make the mistakes I make until I change. I want to begin to change right now.

I am accepting myself by remembering I am a fallible human being, just as good, just as worthwhile as other people.

Sometimes people do what I'm not expecting them to do. Sometimes it seems as if they do not care.

This is my interpretation of their behavior and I could be mistaken. However, even if it is true that some people are inconsiderate of me, and don't really care about how I feel, I still do not have to get upset about it.

Other people have the right to do what they do and to think what they think. They do not have to care about me in order for me to be calm or even happy. Other people's thoughts do not control or define my feelings; other people's actions do not control or define my feelings.

I am a person with human dignity no matter what other people think of me. Even if they don't think of me the way I would like, I can stand it.

I don't need the approval or caring of others in order to feel good about myself. I am the most important person in my life because I control my life.

I control my thoughts, feelings, and behavior. I feel good about the things I do well and regret some things I don't do well. I accept all those behaviors and accept myself.

I feel calm about myself; I feel acceptable to myself; I feel good about accepting myself".

Adapted from Rational Behavior Therapy Center, © Maxie C. Maultsby Jr., M.D., 1978, 2103 Nicholasville Road; Suite 1, Lexington, Kentucky 40503.

The Art of Love

Wilferd A. Peterson

The spectrum of love merges and focuses all of the arts of living.
Friendship, awareness, and happiness, all are the arts of the good life,
are brilliant beads strung on the gold cords of love.
LOVE is the foundation and the apex of the pyramid of our existence.
LOVE is the affirmative of affirmatives; it enlarges the vision and
expands the heart.
LOVE is dynamic motivation behind every worthy purpose;
LOVE is the upward thrust that lifts us to the heights.
LOVE is the creative fire, the inspiration that keeps the torch of
progress aflame.

LOVE penetrates the mysteries of life.

"Anything," said George Washington Carver, "will give up its secrets if you love it enough."

LOVE is the dove of peace, the spirit of brotherhood;

LOVE is tenderness and compassion, forgiveness and tolerance.

LOVE is the supreme good; it is the overflowing life,

The giving of ourselves to noble ends and causes

LOVE is down to earth and it reaches to the highest star;

It is the valley of humility and the mountaintop of ecstasy.

LOVE is the spiritual magnetism that draws people together for the working of miracles.

"Ten men banded together in love," wrote Carlyle, "can do what ten thousand separately would fail in."

LOVE is the perfect antidote that floods the mind to wash away hatred, jealousy, resentment, anxiety, and fear.

LOVE alone can release the power of the atom so it will work for man and not against him.

LOVE, in the words of the Master, is the shinning commandment: Love One Another.

The Art of Love is SPIRIT at work through you.

Chapter 4
The Pillars of a Good Relationship

The best kind of relationships are those that give you a sense of wholeness, security, safety, and a feeling that you are nourished, cared for, and thought of. Where there is even exchange of giving and receiving energy. Sometimes out of our desperation to be loved, we latch on to people whose words do not match their actions. Love is a verb, an "action". Remember to watch what people do, not what they say. Beautiful words stated by the wrong person will bring you heartache and grief. Love is a giving activity. There are many people who will say they love you, who have no idea of what love is, or know how to give love. It is because they themselves have never received love, therefore are void of love, or they are "users" who only know how to take, but not give of their energy, time, attention, caring, or concern. Everything is all them. They are "Me" parasites who only wants to devour their victims, which causes undue suffering and emotional pain.

Suffering occurs when you become attached to expecting more in a relationship than what would give you true happiness. Suffering can be the same in the work you do or in the relationships you have. What makes you sufficiently happy in work is having an opportunity to do work that you enjoy doing. What makes you sufficiently happy in relationships is having an opportunity to love and relate with those you love. Focusing on doing work you enjoy will lead to success and abundance. Focusing on being happy with others and experiencing your love for them when there is an opportunity to do so, will lead you to find those who love you as you are. Happiness is found in enjoying what shows up in your space in the moment. It is the path of least resistance, and it is the path to move through life with ease, peace, and harmony.

You do not hurt a love that loves you and you do not love a love that hurts you. If loving a person makes you happy, it is the right person to love. If loving a person gives you more suffering than joy, it is the wrong person to love. Divine love can and should be given to everyone. Personal love is a sacred thing that is not to be given away to the wrong person or in the wrong place. When love is given to the wrong person or in the wrong place, it contracts and becomes repressed. When love is given to the right person in the right place, love expands and multiplies. Love should bring you joy, contentment, ease, comfort, happiness, and fun as you give and receive from the other person or thing.

What are you looking for when you say you want love? Are you looking for:
• Support (Trust)
• Acceptance (Recognition)
• Validation (Self-Worth)
• Nurturance (Needed)
• Self-Esteem (Feeling of Importance)
• Self-Appreciation (Approval)
• Security (Provided for/Survival)
• Spiritual Wellness (Connected to a Power greater than you)
• Happier Relationships (Connections)
• The validation you have always wanted and never received
• The lover you never had and ache to have

Finding Love Inside Oneself

The law of the universe is love. We are made perfect in this law when we enter into conscious communion with the object of our love. Love is the fulfillment of the law; that is, it is only through love that the law of the universe can fulfill itself in your experience, because love harmonizes and unifies everything. Love gives itself to everything, because it flows through everything. We can never be without love for the very essence of who are is love.

Love does not hurt us, neither does it make us feel bad. And if a person loves us, they share the love inside themselves with us. They will radiate a warm glow of peace and tranquility from the inner core of their being. Love does not hurt us, nor does it abuse us. Love is about freedom, peace, joy, and happiness.

People who love themselves are secure within themselves, and they have a reservoir of loving energy to share. They are not stingy with their love, because they realize that love springs forth from them in a neverending fountain of inner well being. It is a love from the Divine impulse of the universe that keeps replenishing itself on an hourly basis inside us.

LOVE

~ Unknown

Love enough and love will give you wings;
it will cushion the rough places in your road, ease the strains of life,
straightening the way before you, to make effortless the tasks, erasing the drudgery,
Replace it with pleasantness.
Refuse to harbor any feeling other than love.
Your body cannot be out of ease, diseased, while love fills your mind and heart.
You will be fearless for perfect love casts out fear.
You will be happy, for disharmony cannot enter where love is.
You will become beloved, for like attracts like, and love is the greatest attracting power.
You will never be lonely, for love peoples your world with loving companions.
You will never be sad, for love is the greatest happiness maker.
You will be alive, alert, and aware, for love sharpens all faculties.
You will be successful, for love never fails.
Love with every atom of your energy, and no other task will be required of you.
Fill your mind and heart with love to overflowing, and life will pour out its richest blessings upon you.

Love does not consist in gazing at each other, but in looking outward together in the same direction.

Learn To Live the Life You Desire and Deserve

You can program your subconscious mind to create the life you desire and deserve. Each and every moment of your day there is abundant opportunity for you to move from a place of yearning to a place of love, deserving, and abundance. The tools you use to create better outcomes in your life are the same tools you have been using all your life: they are: language, imagination, and emotion.

Whatever your mind is focused on—both consciously and unconsciously—is the reality you create for yourself and those around you. Yet, most of the time, you are programming the subconscious 90% of your mind to create a life that is unfulfilling, that lacks choices, and is filled with pained communication.

Your language directs your thinking. Whatever you are contemplating or thinking you create more of. Through language, we create our own personal Heaven or Hell. If your internal dialogue is, "I'm not good enough. I'm a fool. I did this wrong. My Mom said that about me, and I believe it's the truth!" you will create a reality based on this dialogue. Your subconscious mind does not discriminate. And the outside world will give you evidence of whatever it is your subconscious mind is asking for.

In the privacy of your home, you can learn how to recognize and correct the language patterns—both your internal self-talk and external communication with others—that have been holding you back. By changing the language of your mind, you change the reality of your past, present, and future.

Everyone has the ability to do this. Anyone can learn, because my approach is holistic and personal. My self-help products will teach you proven methods for finding the love, joy, prosperity, and lasting spiritual wellness you have been seeking but did not know how to achieve.

All world religions say that man and woman are made in the image and likeness of Spirit. Cultures from around the world agree that whatever this power is, it is creative in nature. This presupposes that we, too, are creative by nature, as we are made in the image and likeness of this power. Now, my big question to you is, do you think it would be worthwhile to find out how you actually create? NLP is the quickest way to program the most infinite power on the planet: your own human mind.

Dr. Steven Covey says you should ask four questions of yourself:

> What is it that I am really good at?
> What is it I really love to do?
> What need can I serve?
> What is life asking of me?

When have you tapped into your mind and your talent, you'll discover what you're good at. Your heart is your passion (what you love doing). The physical side is your economic need that you're serving in society and this drives your economic engine. And your spiritual side has to do with what does your conscience tells you to do in a given circumstance or situation.

If you can overlap those four things, I feel you can find your inner voice. My experience with most entrepreneurs is that they have found their voice in that way, although sometimes they have not. Sometimes they're beleaguered and beat up. I think that they are so turned on, but the problem is they don't often surround themselves with people who think differently. These people can compensate for their weakness to where they appreciate their voice, so that they create kind of a harmonious chorus, as it were, of people who really know how to work together in the use of their voices.

The Art of Communication

Saying exactly what you're thinking and feeling all the time is NOT a leading trait that makes for a great communicator— or even a good one. Being in touch with your feelings is good. But throwing them out when they come to you, not "filtering" them, and putting no conscious thought behind how the other person will hear and receive your words, is counterproductive.

Tons of women spend days, weeks, or months analyzing, processing, and discussing a thought or idea that they have about a man or about their relationship. Then after all this, they come to a conclusion and present their thoughts to their guy. And then what happens? Most of the time, the woman expects the man to listen and **very quickly** understand what she is talking about, what it means about him and their relationship, and how it makes her feel and why.

And how does that usually work out? If you think about this situation for a second, you'll realize a few important things: The man did not have the benefit of all the time and discussion/analysis that the woman had. The woman was expecting her communication to give him a perfect view and experience of what it's like to be her. The man probably sees things differently and has his own perspective (right or wrong).

Recognize the challenge that you, as a woman, have with a man, it is often very difficult to know what is going on with a man because he will rarely, if ever, come out and say exactly how he is thinking or feeling.

A Credo For Your Relationship With Others

Thomas Gordon, Ph. D

You and I are in a relationship which I value and want to keep. Yet each of us is a separate person with his/her own unique needs and the right to meet those needs. When you are having problems meeting your needs, I will try to listen with genuine acceptance in order to facilitate your finding your own solutions instead of depending on mine. I also will try to respect your right to choose your own beliefs and develop your own values, different though they may be from mine.

However, when your behavior interferes with what I must do to get my own needs met, I will openly and honestly tell you how your behavior affects me, trusting that you respect my needs and feelings enough to try to change the behavior that is unacceptable to me. Also, whenever some behavior of mine is unacceptable to you, I hope you will openly and honestly tell me your feelings. I will then listen and try to change my behavior.

At those times when we find that either of us cannot change his/her behavior to meet the other's needs, let us acknowledge that we have a conflict-of-needs that requires resolving. Let us then commit ourselves to resolve each such conflict without either of us resorting to the use of power or authority to try to win at the expense of the other losing. I respect your needs, but I also must respect my own. So let us always strive to search for a solution that will be acceptable to both of us. Your needs will be met, but so will mine—neither will lose, both will win.

In this way, you can continue to develop as a person through satisfying your needs, but so can I. Thus, ours can be a healthy relationship in which each of us can strive to become what he/she is capable of being. And we continue to relate to each other with mutual respect, love, and peace.

Goals for Improving Your Relationship

If you have decided to stay and work on a relationship that is difficult—even painful or abusive—then it is important to be clear about what needs to change and how you plan to make those changes happen. A couple of things to keep in mind:

• You cannot make your partner change. You can let your partner know what changes you plan to make and what changes you would like him/her to make, but it is up to your partner to decide whether he/she will change or not.

• You are not responsible for your partner's actions. If your partner is abusive, changing your behavior will not make the abuse stop.

Start with listing what you've tried that has **not** worked to improve your relationship in the past.

_____
_____
_____
_____
_____

Now list what **has** worked to improve the relationship in the past.

_____
_____
_____
_____

What are the things that **must** change in order for you to continue this relationship?

_____
_____
_____
_____
_____

Now set a goal for those changes to happen:

_____
_____
_____
_____
_____

Who is responsible for making this goal happen?

_____

What are the steps that will need to be taken to achieve this goal?

_____
_____
_____
_____
_____
_____

When will you reevaluate this goal to see if it has been achieved?

_____

What will happen if the goal is reached?

_____
_____
_____
_____
_____

Areas of Conflict in Communicating as a Couple

This information is designed for couples who are committed to their relationships and interested in improving the quality of their interaction. Some common areas of conflict in couple communications are:

1. **How to talk** about your problems and feelings without arousing your partner's anger or defensiveness.

2. **How to listen** to your partner's problems and feelings without becoming angry and defensive yourself.

3. **How to resolve conflicts** when both you and your partner have talked and listened and find you disagree.

4. **How to handle anger** constructively and prevent arguments from escalating.

How to Communicate With a Partner

A lot of couples begin a communication program or class with both secretly (and not so secretly) believing that their problems are caused in large part by their partners. Each person sees himself or herself as the mostly innocent victim of the other person's bad behavior, and each person hopes that the class will get the partner to change: to listen, to express feelings, or to stop nagging and criticizing.

Because this is a common expectation, I want to emphasize what a communication class can and can't provide. Neither the class nor you can change your partner. Who you *can* change is *yourself*: how you behave, how you communicate, and how you solve problems. As you wonder how to get your relationship to change, you realize that you hold one of the most important keys: your own behavior. You are incredibly powerful influence on your relationship.

You may say, "I have tried to change myself and it didn't work. It's about time for my partner to do some changing." That may well be true, but the fact remains that the most effective way to bring about change in a relationship is to change yourself. Both of you need to swallow your pride, to take the first step, and take the attitude: "I'm going to learn these skills; I'm going to respond differently." Even if it occasionally feels like giving in to the other person, the formal research with couples has shown that it is in your personal self-interest, not just for the good of the relationship, to learn these skills for yourself.

Some Communication Patterns to Recognize and Avoid

1. **The Summarizing Self Syndrome**
   Both people keep restating their own positions. Nobody listens to anyone else. The conversation sounds like this:
   " Blah, blah."
   "Yak, yak."
   "What I said was blah, blah."
   "Didn't you hear me say yak. Yak?"....and so on.

2. **Kitchen Sink-ing**
   People start out discussing one issue but then drift into other topics. They often end up dragging "everything but the kitchen sick" into the conversation. Pretty soon both people get the feeling that they have to deal with all of the issues at once.

3. **Yes, But.....**
   Every time one person makes a suggestion, the other person finds something wrong with it. Partners sometimes are not aware of this habit.

4. **Cross Complaining**
   Person A makes a complaint or request of person B. Person B doesn't respond to the issue; instead, B brings up a complaint about A.

5. **Mind Reading**
   One person assumes knowledge of what the other person is "really" thinking or wanting.

6. **Interrupting**

Not allowing the person to express their opinion

7. **Insulting Your Partner**
   Saying demeaning or unkind words

8. **Threatening Your Partner-**
   Making the person feel scared or that their life is   in danger.

9. **Airing Old Resentments**
   Bringing up old hurts or resentments from the   past

10. **Being Vague**
    People speak in generalities without giving specifics. For example, "You're driving funny today."

11. **Over-generalizing-**These statements usually begin with "You never…" or "You always…"

Assumptions and Skills for Effective Communication

The first basic assumption is that feelings, *all kinds of feelings exist.* Feelings are not good or bad, wrong or right, correct or incorrect, they are **just feelings.** The second assumption is that all of us have the right to have any feeling in the world. Some behaviors or actions may need to be limited, but *any feeling* is **okay.** And each of us is the ***ultimate authority*** on our own feelings. No one can tell you what you feel or don't feel. Another person may not like what you are feeling or may feel differently. But no one can tell you that you don't feel the way you do. The third assumption is that an intimate relationship, at its best, is a place where both partners feel safe to share feelings, when they choose to, without getting attacked for doing so. To build that kind of relationship, you need two sets of communications skills. One set is *speaking,* and one is for *listening.* Both skills are essential.

Skills for Speaking

Use "I-messages". An "I" message is a sentence that starts with the word "I" and expresses a feeling. Here is why an "I-message" is more effective than a "you-message". Suppose X says to Y, "You play too much golf." Y can protest, "I do not." Y feels attacked and put down and is tempted to retaliate with a counterattack. But if X says to Y, "I feel jealous when you play golf," Y cannot say, "You do not." X is taking responsibility for his/her own feelings, and no one can say that X doesn't, or shouldn't, fell that way.

To communicate what you are feeling, you need to *know* what you are feeling. This takes practice. It involves getting to know your body and the signals it gives to tell you what you are feeling. It also involves becoming familiar with the typical pattern of thoughts that go along with specific feelings for you. To help you start this process, use the sample feeling chart below. When you want to know what you are feeling, you might look at the chart and select the word that best approximates how you feel at the moment

Positive

Willing	Content	Turned on		
Calm	Secure	Loving	Ready	
Warm	Strong	Bubbly	Interested	
Sexy	Happy	Peaceful	Ambitious	Excited
	Busy	Confident	Imaginative	

I feel....
A Little   **Somewhat**   **Very**......

Negative

Grouchy	Ashamed	Silly	Sorry	
Sad	Bored	Hurt	Sully	
Anxious	Alone	Shy	Rebellious	
Tired	Dumb	Guilty	Confused	
Nervous	Trapped	Frustrated	Listless	

Restless   Put down   Ignored   Depressed

When you speak in I-statements, you don't have to use complicated feeling words. Someone once said that there are four basic feelings, and three of them rhyme: mad, sad, glad, and afraid. If you're ever not sure what you're feeling, scan those four. Other useful feeling phrases are:

I like it when ….
I don't like it when…
I want….
I wish….

Sometimes our feelings have two parts; for example, "*I want* to go, but I *don't want* to spend the money." This is a perfectly legitimate I-statement, so when you feel two things, say both of them.

Other Do's and Don'ts for effective speaking:

> Do own your feelings. For example, "I get mad."
> Do be specific when you feel that way. For example, "I get mad when clothes are on the bathroom floor."
> Do say directly what you want. For example: "I'd like you to take them out of the bathroom."
> Don't ask questions.
> Don't judge, preach, criticize, or blame.
> Don't use name calling.
> Don't interpret, diagnose, or analyze.

Here is a formula you can use to build an I-message when you want to give your partner feedback about his/her behavior.

> "When you do....X... (Describe the behavior), I feel...Y."
>
> And if you want change, add:
>
> "I would prefer...Z." (Describe the behavior)

Relationship Skills for Listening to Others

Your partner's I-messages are wasted if you don't hear them. Therefore, good communication requires using a skill called **validating** or **active listening**. Active listening means **hearing your partner** and communicating to him/her that if you are seeing things his/her way, with his/her assumptions, it would be reasonable to feel that way.

The essence of active listening is to express empathy with your partner's feelings, while preserving a neutral, non-judgmental stance yourself. It is not necessary to share or agree with your partner's feelings in order to empathize with them. It is also not necessary to solve his or her problem or to offer advice or suggestions.

In active listening you paraphrase the content and reflect back the feeling or meaning behind your partner's words. This shows your partner that his/her feelings are heard and understood. It encourages your partner to make his/her own I-statements, and it thereby sets the stage for later negotiations. It also tends to defuse your partner's opposition and to create a positive, caring atmosphere.

Other Do's and Don'ts for Effective Listening Validation:

Do remember the basic assumption that every person has the right to any feeling in the world
Do put your own feelings "on a back burner" while you are the "listener". Later, when you are the "speaker", you will have a

chance to express your feelings, and your partner will listen to you.

Don't say or imply that your partner "shouldn't feel that way".

Don't express your feelings—of disagreement or agreement—or make suggestions at this point.

Don't interpret what you think your partner "really feels".

Don't try to get your partner to change his or her mind.

Some Examples of Active Listening

"It sounds like you want it too but are worried about how we'll be able to pay for it."

"What I'm hearing you say is that my not checking with you first caused you a lot of embarrassment."

"Your first choices are to go out for pizza, second choice is to grill hamburgers at home, and you really don't want to go out for chicken. Did I get that right?"

"Let me check out if I'm hearing you accurately. What you minded wasn't so much that the house was dirty, but you felt that I didn't care enough to clean it.'

"You're saying you really like it when we snuggle up on the sofa."

How To Listen And Hear

Anon

When I ask you to listen to me and you start giving advice you have not done what I asked.

When I ask you to listen to me and you begin to tell me why I shouldn't feel that way, you are trampling on my feelings.

When I ask you to listen to me and you feel you have to do something to solve my problem, you have failed me, strange as that may seem.

Listen! All I asked was that you listen. Not to talk or do—just hear me.

Advice is cheap: 10 cents will get you both Dear Abby and Billy Graham in the same newspaper.

And I can do for myself; I'm not helpless, maybe discouraged and faltering, but not helpless.

When you do something for me that I can and need to do for myself, you contribute to my fear and weakness.

But, when you accept as a simple fact that I do feel what I feel, no matter how irrational, then I can quit trying to convince you and can get about the business of understanding what's behind this irrational feeling. And when that's clear, the answers are obvious and I don't need advice.

Irrational feelings make sense when we understand what is behind them

Perhaps that's why prayer works, sometimes, for some people because Spirit is mute, and He doesn't give advice or try to fix things. "They" just listen and let you work it out for yourself.

So, please listen and just hear me. And, if you want to talk, wait a minute for your turn and I will listen to you.
          Anon

Soft Assertion Skills

"Soft assertion" means speaking up about your warm, positive feelings toward each other. It is dangerous to assume that your spouse knows you appreciate him/her when he/she does something special. **Say It.** Even routine behaviors are more likely to happen again if they are acknowledged.

Rules to Follow:

Be as specific as you can in acknowledging positive behavior.

1. Describe, don't evaluate, for example: Do say: "The spaghetti is delicious tonight."
   Don't say, "You're such a wonderful cook."

2. Avoid global generalizations of all kinds such as, "You, always do such a great job," "I can always count on you," etc. (These statements are often embarrassing to the recipient and are usually discounted.)

3. Acknowledge attempts and/or partially completed tasks by commenting on what
   is done well. Don't wait for perfection or total success.

4. Even if it seems obvious, **SAY IT!** One kind word produces another. You'll be surprised how fast a positive cycle can be generated and what far-reaching effects it can have on the whole relationship.

5. When you receive a compliment, say "THANK YOU." Don't apologize or disqualify it.

Do This to Ask For a Request For Change

A request for change should be:
   1. Positive
   2. Specific
   3. Small

4. Not the subject of a recent conflict

Examples: Do not say, "I wish you'd quit being such a slob." (Negative and general) "I wish you'd be neater." (Positive, but too vague)

Do say, "I'd really appreciate it if you'd hang up your towel after you use it." (Positive, specific, and small)

Relationship Skills are Essential In Every Area of Your Life

The skills you need to develop or improve your relationships are often a test to determine if you are ready for success in your relationships with others.

1. Know what you want (intention).
2. People connections strengthen your personality.
3. Know your personal strengths and weaknesses.
4. Get a good supporting network of quality friends
5. Have relationship goals for yourself
6. Have an action plan to accomplish your relationship goals, who you want to meet, what character traits you have/want to match, and when do you want this to happen?
7. Be willing to state your relationship non negotiation rules

Impediments to Collaborate or Connect with Others:
1. Fear of connection
2. Fear of commitment/Impatience.
3. Fear of Rejection

What Makes a Woman Successful?

The successful woman knows herself well and uses her talents wisely. With warmth in her smile and comfort in her touch,

She lets others know how special they are.
She thinks children are priceless, and all nature is precious,
And asks what she can do, to make the world a safer, better place.
The successful woman is not looking for success...
It finds her while she is reaching out, touching herself with others.

I Release and I Let Go

Rickie Byars Beckwith

I release and I let go, I let the Spirit run my life,
And my heart is open wide, yes I'm only here for Spirit.
No more struggle, no more strife, with my faith I see the light,
I am free in the Spirit, yes I'm only here for Spirit.
I release and I let go, I let the Spirit run my life,
And my heart is open wide, yes I'm only here for Spirit.
No more struggle, no more strife, with my faith I see the light,
I am free in the Spirit", yes I'm only here for Spirit.

Ideal Lover/Partner Traits and Qualities

Much of the time a Partner/Committed Lover:
— Is nurturing
— Is flexible
— Is understanding
— Is consistent
— Allows growth
— Acknowledges you as a unique individual
— Accepts and approves of who you are, and does not want to change you or make you over to be the person they want
— Is Attentive
— Wants to Be Involved in Your Life
— Open to Guidance/Corrective Feedback
— Open to Have Better Communication

- Comfortable with Your Faults & Flaws
- Can Give Validation
- Is Flexible
- Understanding
- Value Personal Growth
- Is Cooperative
- Listens without judgment
- Is accepting
- Is Kind and Considerate
- Knows how to let go (is not possessive)
- Establishes and maintains routines as needed
- Is an ally/Friend
- Models wholeness and balance
- Knows the difference between love and non-love touching
- Appreciate Consistency
- Likes Structure
- Gives Positive Reinforcement
- Builds Confidence in the other person
- Has Realistic Expectations
- Is Lovable
- Has Good Coping Skills
- Is Hopeful, Has a Positive Outlook on the Relationship/Life
- Is Trusting and Trust -Worthy
- Makes times for Their Partner and their Relationship
- Has His or Her Frustrations, Irritations and Anger Under Control of the time

Live Life to the Fullest: A Guide to Self-Esteem

Anon

Don't let go of hope. Hope gives you the strength to keep going when you feel like giving up.
Don't ever quit believing in yourself.

As long as you believe you can,
You will have a reason for trying.
Don't let anyone hold your happiness in their hands;
Hold it in yours, so it will always be within your reach
Don't measure success or failure by material wealth,
But by how you feel;
Our feelings determine the richness or our lives.
Don't let bad moments overcome you;
Be patient and they will pass.
Don't hesitate to reach out for help;
We all need it from time to time.
Don't run away from love but towards love, because it is our deepest
joy.
Don't wait for what you want to come to you.
Go after it with all that you are, knowing that life will meet you halfway
Don't feel like you have lost, when plans and dreams fall short of your
hopes;
Anytime you learn something new about yourself or about life you have
progressed.
Don't do anything that takes away from your self-respect.
Feeling good about yourself is essential to feeling good about life.
Don't ever forget how to laugh or be too proud to cry.
It is by doing this that we live life to its fullest.

The Prayer of St. Francis of Assisi

Lord, make me an instrument of your peace.
Where there is hatred, let me sow love;
Where there is injury, pardon;
Where there is doubt, faith;
Where there is despair, hope;
Where there is darkness, light;
Where there is sadness, joy.
Oh divine master, grant that I may not so much seek to

Be consoled as to console;
To be understood, as to understand;
To be loved, as to love;
For it is in giving, that we receive;
It is in pardoning, that we are pardoned;
And it is in dying, that we area born to eternal life.

Leave Trails for Others to Follow

Traditions That are timeless, which pass our faith to the next generation.

Roots That are rich in heritage, that will firmly develop our children's spiritual and moral character.

Attitudes which are Angelic in nature,

Inspiration to build a bridge for others to cross,

A Legacy of Love for our sons and daughters and

Strength to continue the journey

Motivational Reminders

Motivation fuels the fire within. Again, attitude about life's setbacks and not the setbacks themselves determine success.

1. Once you make a choice, it then makes you.

2. In order for change to occur on the outside, it must first occur on the inside.

3. Choosing today, changes tomorrow.

4. Successful people fail more than failures do.

5. You will miss 100% of the shots you don't take.

6. Knowledge enables, empowers, and endorses success.

7. There are few feelings greater than feeling that we control our desires, rather than allowing our desires to control us.

8. Your strengths are seen in what you stand for, your weaknesses in what you fall for.

9. A temporary commitment cannot solve a long-term problem.

10. If you don't control your life, your life will control you.

11. Learn to experience the momentary pain of discipline, rather than the lasting pain of regret.

12. You can't change where you've been, but you can change where you're going.

13. People generally fail, not because they're defeated, but because they quit.

14. You were not created to fail; you were created to succeed.

15. Your work will pay off; it's not a matter of if, but when.

16. The goal you set today will be the reward you receive tomorrow.

17. Success lies in your ability to look beyond the challenge and focus on the goal.

18. If you don't schedule your time, time will schedule you.

19. Physical and spiritual fitness provide the energy to deal with life's challenges, the strength to press through, and the ability to continue regardless of circumstances.

20. Poor choices take us farther than we want to go, keep us longer than we want to stay, and cost us more that we want to pay.

21. Don't get discouraged. It's not the fall that hurts; it's staying down that does.

22. Success is determined by the ability to take action, failure by the inability to take action.

23. Desire will find a way; excuses hide the way.

24. Thoughts become words, words become actions, actions become habits, and habits become a lifestyle.

25. Putting first things first leads to success.

26. Take the safest route, not the fastest.

27. Those who succeed walk through adversity, not without it.

28. Success in weight loss is 10% circumstance, 90% attitude.

29. Never look back unless it's the direction you want to go.

30. A true measure of a person is not what they were, but what they will become.

31. The obstacles ahead are never as great as the power behind.

32. Don't let someone's opinion of you become your reality.

33. Your life is a reflection of the choices you make.

34. Keep moving forward despite obstacles.

Love is a lot like a competition,
With Its ups and downs,
And all you have to do to win
Is rise each time you fall!

Angels on the Wing

Anon

When you feel abandoned from life's every good thing, don't forget the comfort brought by Angels on The Wing.

As the artist weds himself to beauty, imbibing the essence or spirit of beauty that it may be transmitted to the canvas or awaken the cold marble to living form, so you must wed yourself to love. You must imbibe its spirit. This love is more than a sentiment. It is a deep sense of the underlying unity and beauty of all life, the goodness running through everything, the giving-ness of life to everything. Say:

Today I bestow the essence of love upon everything.

Everyone shall be lovely to me.

My soul meets the soul of the universe in everyone.

Everything is beautiful, everything is meaningful.

This love is a healing power touching everything into wholeness, healing the wounds of experience with its divine balm.

I know that this love essence is the very substance of life, the creative principle back of everything, flowing through my whole being, spiritual, emotional, mental, and physical.

It flows in transcendent loveliness into my world of thought and form, ever renewing, vitalizing, bringing joy, harmony, and blessing to everything and everyone it touches.

You are to know that good keeps you in perfect activity, surrounds you with love and friendship, and brings the experience of joy to everything you do.

Our Thoughts Are Prayers

Lucille K. Olson

Our thoughts are prayers
And we are always praying
Our thoughts are prayers
Be careful what you're saying
Seek a higher consciousness
A state of peacefulness
And know that Spirit is always there
And every thought becomes a prayer.

LOVE

Anon

Love may sometimes be a light thing
You may wear it like a flower
Or a ring upon your finger
Yet love has lasting power.
But whether love lights lightly
Or for eternity,
You find the more it binds you,
The more it sets you free.
Love may sometimes lay a heavy load
You think you cannot bear,
But love and you together
Have strength enough to spare.
Love lifts you on invisible
But ah, what mighty wings!
When life is dearest and most blessed,
Love is the song it sings.

Never talk defeat. Use words like hope, belief, faith, victory.

Life's blows cannot break a person whose spirit is warmed at the fire of enthusiasm.

It is of practical value to learn to like you. Since you must spend so much time with yourself, you might as well get some satisfaction out of the relationship.

Develop a tremendous faith in Spirit and that will give you a humble yet soundly realistic faith in yourself.

Miracles are of all sizes. And if you start believing in little miracles, you can work up to the bigger ones.

Chapter 5
How to Find the Love You Want

According to Fenny Smedley, life therapist, angel intuitive, author of 20 books, and award-winning lyricist, most people automatically think in terms of a partner, chemistry, a life-long union, so they are often disappointed because this is not always the case. Also many people believe that there is only one soul mate for them in the entire world. This is inaccurate too. It's possible to have many different soul mates of different kinds. What kinds of soul mates are there? There are opinions on how many kinds of soul mates there are, everywhere you look, but my experience has made me believe in four main kinds:

Eternal Flames: This is what most people picture when they think of perfect soul mates. This is someone who feels like half of you. Whenever they're absent, your life almost seems to go on hold. They know what you are thinking and they offer you total unconditional love. There will be no battlefields with them; only maybe minor skirmishes as both parties have to learn their own lessons, but the partnership embodies the saying that together, two people are greater than the sum of their parts. There will be no unfaithfulness, because the love these people feel goes down to a soul level, and it will be impossible for them to hurt each other, and they will never desire any other person. Not everyone will find this kind of soul mate in every life they live. Because of the strong dependency that can be formed, this is not always a good thing, and it might not be right at this particular stage of their existence. Because of this we may live some lifetimes apart from our Eternal Flame, just to make sure that we learn to rely on ourselves and not on someone else.

Twin Soul Mates: One step down, in a way, from Eternal Flames, this can be the most confusing type of soul mate of all, because love is certainly and obviously there between them. They can be very alike in many ways, and they seem familiar right from their first meeting—and they are familiar, because you will always have known them before, in other lifetimes. They make you feel comfortable, because in a past life they were probably your friend or partner, and it's tempting to think you can just take up where you left off with them. It is an instinctual pull, and sometimes it is right. But this is where the trouble can come, because often they are just there to help you out, and often not meant to be your lifelong partner. Not realizing this, and perhaps being pressured to commit by social peers, you might marry this twin soul and then further down the line find you need to part. Or you can be meant to be partners for a short time, perhaps to create specific children, and once those children have been created the need to be together disappears.

Teacher Soul Mates: There is a saying: "When the pupil is ready, the teacher will appear." Soul mates of this kind will sometimes come into our lives, usually temporarily, to enable us to learn something vital to our soul's progress. They will not normally be a partner, but this can happen. The relationship can be challenging and difficult. And the lesson can be harsh. However, once the lesson has been given, this person will sometimes vanish as mysteriously as they appeared, and this can cause us to feel upset and confused.

Comforter Soul Mates: They can step into your life, sometimes to just say a specific word, or do a certain thing, or bring comfort and companionship when you're feeling alone, or offer some advice to help you make a tricky decision. They are often lifelong friends once they appear. They think the same way as you and are always there for you, but you never see them as a potential partner. They are often the opposite sex, and yet there is no sexual chemistry between the two of you. This is a true platonic relationship.

Love is Something You Do; It Is Action

Love is not a noun. It involves your taking some action if you want to find love or be in a loving relationship. Listed below are some actions you will need to take to increase your chances of finding the love you want. They are: Respect, Accountability, Accommodation, Reciprocity, Compromise, and Mutuality.

Respect: Showing the type of respect in my words and actions that reflects how I wish to be respected and in turn, shows how I respect myself (i.e., setting personal boundaries in a healthy, assertive manner).

Accountability: Taking responsibility for my own verbal and non-verbal behaviors in the relationship, particularly those verbal and non-verbal behaviors that are hurtful to another person, or do I use some form of self-protection that deflects responsibility for my behaviors to some other source (i.e., become contemptuous, become defensive, become critical, or stonewall).

Accommodation: Making room/space for a partner or giving of myself for a partner (i.e., living together, becoming an interdependent couple, both the "we" and the individual "me" as part of the sharing in a partner's interest if the partner desires this).

Reciprocity: It is giving behaviors in a relationship. You want to be careful to avoid keeping score or expecting something in return. If you want ease in your relationship, give for the sake of giving because it gives you joy to please your partner.

Compromise: Being able to reach an agreement that is acceptable to both partners whether this agreement involves choosing to support/accept one partner's wishes, or finding the middle ground, or agreeing to disagree.

Mutuality: Working as a team to solve a problem, creating mutually agreed on goals for the future, and finding commonalities that defines you as a couple rather than individuals in a relationship.

The Five Languages of Love
Here are the five primary ways we give and receive love according to author Gary Chapman:
• Words of affirmation
• Quality time
• Gifts
• Acts of service
• Physical touch

The Many Faces of Love

We tend to forget that life, no matter what aspect of living we may be focused on, is about our evolution. Our earthling mind may forget this great truth, but our "Soul" would never let such important information be overlooked—not even for a minute. It is because your SOUL has come directly from Source/Spirit/The Creator, and absolutely understands this, for it is a cornerstone of creation. Therefore, your Soul would also understand that the *reason* for having a "Soul Lover" or a "Soul Mate" is for your shared evolution, and the express purpose is so that the two of you can facilitate each other's growth.

But there is much more to a soul connection than that, and that's where Spirit comes in to guide you to the right person. Spirit teaches you not only how to recognize and harvest the wonderful growth that you and your Soul Mate(s) will be generating for each other, but also how to love that growth and still love each other. It also teaches how to keep expanding that growth, use that growth to achieve your destiny, and have fun together doing it or not doing it. Some soul lessons may not be fun, but are necessary for your soul's evolution.

This is only possible when you live your "Soul's Intelligence", when you are open to receive inner guidance from your High Self or Divine Self. When you receive the "Inner Guidance" to understand, you surrender your will to the Divine and open your heart to be open to receive lover. When you allow this illumined understanding to empower your growth, then your spiritual growth will allow you to step all the way into your life's destiny.

You Deserve Love

Ultimately love is self-approval.

Love is the place you are coming from, your ground of being. You are love.

Love is the divine force everywhere, the universal energy, the moving power of life that flows in your own heart.

Love is accepting someone as he or she is and as he or she is not.

Love is the acknowledgement of a union that already exists.

You already are part of this universal unifying essence called love. In addition, you are either loving or not loving. If you are a loving person, people will feel your attractive force and will appear in your path so you can love them. And there are multitudes of people who want to express their love to you. It is important to realize however, that you cannot accept any more love than you are willing to give yourself. Many people have had so much disapproval in life that they have forgotten how to go about loving themselves.

What is Self-Love?

Self-love is acknowledging & praising yourself out loud to yourself.

Self-love is approving of all your actions.

Self-love is having confidence in your ability.

Self-love is giving yourself pleasures without guilt.

Self-love is loving your body and admiring your beauty.

Self-love is giving yourself what you want and feeling you deserve it.

Self-love is letting yourself win.

Self-love is letting others in instead of submitting to loneliness.

Self-love is following your own intuition.

Self-love is making your own rules responsibly.

Self-love is seeing your own perfection.

Self-love is taking credit for what you did.

Self-love is surrounding yourself with beauty,
Self-love is letting yourself be rich and not staying in poverty.
Self-love is creating an abundance of friends.
Self-love is rewarding yourself, never punishing yourself.
Self-love is trusting yourself.
Self-love is nourishing yourself with good food and good ideas.
Self-love is surrounding yourself with people who nourish you.
Self-love is enjoying sex.
Self-love is getting a massage frequently.
Self-love is seeing yourself as equal to others.
Self-love is forgiving yourself and others.
Self-love is letting in affection.
Self-love is authority over yourself, not giving it away to another.
Self-love is developing your creative drives.
Self-love is having fun all the time.
Self-love is really talking to yourself gently and lovingly.
Self-love is becoming your own approving inner parent.
Self-love is turning all your negative thoughts into affirmations.

If you have a good relationship with yourself, you will automatically have a good relationship with others. "The soul attracts that which is secretly harbors." In other words, you will attract the person who has harmony with your thought structures. If you feel really good about yourself, you'll attract someone who feels good about him/herself. By the universal law of attraction, someone will respond to the mental vibrations you exude.

You can create the perfect relationship for yourself by sitting down and listing the things you want in such a relationship. Meditate on them. Imagine already having such a relationship. Imagine the person you want for a partner. If you really are willing for it to happen, someone will come into your life just as you imagine, by this universal law of attraction. Thought creates vibrations which inevitably attract that which is in its image.

If you are already in a relationship, the same procedure will work. Picture these positive, divine qualities coming out in him/her. Your partner will soon develop and become as you imagine. Jesus often spoke of the law of attraction. "As you believe, so shall it be done unto you." "Unto him who hath, shall be given." When you come to understand that there is only one universal mind which is every place at the same time and in all things, you will see that the differences between you are others are illusionary. We are all the same; we are just vibrating at different levels of energy. When you raise your energy vibration level, you will attract people on higher and higher energy levels.

Do not dwell on thoughts of the lack of things. There are no limitations. There is no lack in the universal mind of Spirit in which we are all a part. Whatever you ask for you will be given. However, you must believe and expect that what you want will happen. So watch yourself and watch your thoughts. If you are thinking, "I'll never meet somebody who _____ ", you never will. Immediately invert the thought to something like this: "I am now attracting someone who _____ ".

What you are willing to accept will come your way. Ken Keyes said, "Happiness is experienced when life gives you what you are willing to accept." So take responsibility for the thoughts you choose to think regarding your relationships. You can bring people you like into your life with your thoughts. The logical person to put in your circle is someone with whom you are in harmony or whomever you think you deserve.

Let's say you are now in a caring, fulfilling, loving relationship. You may wonder how to make or keep it successful. It's easy. A successful relationship is based upon one person being nourished by the other person's presence. If you just do that, it's enough. You don't have to do anything else except set up certain agreements you will both keep. You can make it a game, but don't get stuck in the rules of how you think the other should be or act. You might want to change your rules of how to be in a relationship as frequently as every week. Learn to negotiate what you want, need, or choose to have.

Are You Looking to Find Love As a Mother/Wife?

I am still looking at how I can get adults to move into a natural play mode rather in some of the artificial ways that some adults use like alcohol and recreational drugs, which tend to cloud their spirit of play. Children are into natural play, so I do not have to coach them on how to play. They have problems when they are trying to be who they are and learn how to live with a parent who is into an artificial place. It is easy for me to counsel a child on how to live with a crazy parent. For the mom it will take some counseling for her to let go of her artificial form of play (drugs) and later coach her on how to go back to her natural playful child that she has lost. My challenge is how I can get the insurance company to pay for my counseling of her and her child. She has money issues and is now looking for how she can set aside her money to provide for her son in the future. I realize now I that I can get paid to help people solve problems, I want to figure out how to get people to pay me to coach them on how to play or help them re-learn how to play.

These are some insights Christian Carter shares about men and about why men withdraw from a relationship. He says once women understand it will stop a lot of the pain and frustration women experience with dating and relationships. When a man gets truly close to a woman and deeply intimate, for any extended period of time, he loves that feeling and wants more of it. But the strange part of this is that the moment a man experiences this period of intense closeness, he will take some space for himself.

I know this sounds counter-intuitive, but it is how most men work emotionally. Most men will actually seek some amount of space to "recover". It's kind of like how after a muscle gets worked out it needs to rest before it can grow stronger and be active again. Men can become distant even in good relationships, and if you know what to do, you can keep a guy physically and emotionally engaged even when he needs time to recover.

And there's another reason why a man might withdraw that has nothing whatsoever to do with the women; he's not living his "purpose".

The Importance of Purpose For a Man

It's important for a man to be clear about what he's doing in his own life and what his purpose is. A man's purpose can be anything from something straightforward like excelling at work or building his own company, to something more creative like starting and working at a do-it-yourself project at home or training at his favorite sport.

The point is that a man has some goals and is engaged and focused on doing something and doing it well. A man's purpose is essential to his overall emotional and social well-being. But often times, even men themselves aren't clear on what their purpose is, or don't really go after their purpose and assert themselves.

How a Man's Purpose (or Lack of) Can Affect a Woman

When a man isn't going after his own purpose, or has fallen away from it, or forgotten about it, it often gets in the way of the relationship he's in. Men become withdrawn, restless, irritated, and seem generally unengaged in life as a whole. They stop initiating plans. They stop spending as much time with people, even their own friends. They shut the world out. And of course, they become emotionally withdrawn and distant as well.

Too often men aren't conscious that this is what's happening to them, and they end up pulling away from their relationship and making things even worse for themselves. This is when they often seem to go in and out of being present and engaged in the relationship and then completely withdrawn.

They slide between the two largely because of the way that they're feeling about themselves or how things are going for them in the world as it relates to their purpose. And often women take on the problems the man is going through and try and help, or even mistake his behavior to mean something about his feelings about them or the relationship. So, now that we know that a man's withdrawing is not automatically the woman's fault, she can nothing do about it.

What Doesn't Work In Love for Men

There are certain behaviors and approaches women often take when their man starts withdrawing, and they usually work against the woman. Let's get those out of the way so we know what NOT to do...

Approach #1: Convincing Him

If you're a woman, when you're with a man who is feeling or acting uncertain with you, trying to convince him otherwise puts you in a very dangerous and weak position for your relationship, even if you give him an ultimatum that would move things ahead to the place in your relationship that you want. Why? Because he's not really making that decision based on what he wants or feels. What you really want and need is a man who is truly committed to being with you on a physical, mental, emotional, and even spiritual level. Not coerced, not forced, not convinced.

Approach #2: Over Sharing Your Feelings

If you're like most women, then you think sharing your feelings with a man first, and often, will somehow get him to share his feelings in return. But this isn't how it works for a man. You can share your feelings with a man, but to expect that this will encourage him to do the same with you will only lead you to unnecessary frustration, especially if a man is already acting withdrawn. When a man acts withdrawn, that's a signal that he is undergoing his own emotional process and needs time to recharge. Once he's ready to share his feelings, he'll be back. But trying to stimulate him to do so, by becoming overly emotional won't work.

Approach #3: Setting Unrealistic Expectations
Women tend to think that if things are going well with a guy, that he will naturally want to move things forward to the next level. They'll just assume this even when the guy has never talked about the future. So you know what happens next. Things will be coasting along, and suddenly the guy will change gears, she'll find out he's dating other women, or he doesn't make plans with her every weekend, and she's left wondering what the heck happened. The answer is that the woman created all these expectations about what the relationship was supposed to look like and how he was supposed to behave, and when he fell short of that, she became disappointed and unfulfilled. This usually winds up in a confrontation that causes tension and maybe even creates more distance. The flip side of this is that a woman will try to pretend she's okay with just a casual relationship, gets closer to him thinking he'll "come around", and then becomes disappointed when he doesn't.

Approach #4: Having "The Talk"
As an independent thinking woman who is used to getting out there and getting what she wants in her career and the rest of her life, it might seem like laying your cards on the table and having a talk with a man about "where the relationship is going" is the sensible, adult way to move things forward. You might think that if you give him all your reasons for why you two are perfect for each other, like you'd do in a job interview, it will make him open his eyes and realize he'd be a fool to have things any other way. But think about this: Do men truly commit and choose to love and become loyal, caring, affectionate, etc. just because a woman asks them?

No. A man needs to have his own reasons for being and feeling this way, and this happens when he feels a deep emotional attraction for you.

Affirmations to Improve or Change Your Relationships

I _____ (your name) now approve of
_____ (other person's name) and take responsibility
for my feelings of jealousy.

The more freedom I give my partner the more he/ she loves me.

I no longer need _____ (other person's name) for my
survival so it does not matter if he/she has other behavior patterns.

I _____ no longer need to see _____ as
my father/mother and struggle to get his/her love.

I _____ am now willing to let my incestuous feelings
toward my father/mother surface.

I _____ now take responsibility to establish agreements
about outside relationships.

I _____ am careful not to use outside relationships
as a form of manipulation.

I_____ no longer need to set _____ up as
my mother or father.

I.... no longer expect _____ to show love to
me in this manner.

I now let _____ communicate openly in a
harmonious way.

I no longer need the dramatic outbursts I used as a child to get attention, now that I love and accept myself.

Since you have no guarantee that your partner will be faithful, it is better to work on the affirmation "I _____ now approve of _____ and take responsibility for my feelings of jealousy" so you can better handle any feelings of jealousy and take the pressure off your companion.

When your partner notices your approving attitude or behavior, he/she will appreciate it. He/she may be confused at first, because it may be hard for them to believe they are getting the approval they wanted. The game playing will be over because the old payoff will longer be there. Just getting in touch with your underlying purposes in the game playing will help both of you to change. It can be very releasing when you take a more mature approach to your relationship building skills and give yourself an option for outside relationship building, even if it is on a limited basis.

LETTING GO

Anon

LETTING GO does not mean to stop caring; it means not to take responsibility for someone else.

LETTING GO is not to enable others; it is to allow learning from natural consequences.

LETTING GO is to admit my own powerlessness, which means the outcome is not in my hands.

LETTING GO is not to try to change or blame others, but to make the most of myself.

LETTING GO is not to care for, but to care about.

LETTING GO is not to fix, but to be supportive.

LETTING GO is not to be protective; it's to permit another to face reality.

LETTING GO is not to deny, but to accept.

LETTING GO is not to nag, scold, or argue; it is to search out my own shortcomings and correct them.

LETTING GO is not to adjust everything to my desires, but to take each day as it comes and cherish myself in it.

LETTING GO is not to criticize and regulate others, but to grow and live for the future.

LETTING GO is to fear less, and love more.

Our past is always with us even though we modify it with what happens in the present. As I have mentioned, old thought patterns can continue to produce results even though we are no longer thinking them. By the same token, we can still be acting out old relationships even though these people are not present. These truths are revealed to me over and over again when I take a client's sexual history. When I ask that person to describe his/her first childhood sex experience, I see that the conclusions made right after that experience are often still producing results years and years later. And yet, you do not have to stay stuck in the past. If you change the generalizations now that you made in the past, you can, in effect, change the past.

Since we carry our mind with us wherever we go and we produce the same results over and over, it is obvious that it is only when we change our consciousness that we can expect permanent replacements of old negative patterns. This is why affirmations are so powerful. Try repeating some of these to change your frame of mind

My bedroom is no longer a place of punishment.
It is a place of reward

I now forgive my father/mother for hitting, beating, hurting me.

Other men are not my father, and I do not need to fear them.

For the first time in my life I will begin to spend some time relaxing in my bedroom. I have redecorated it in a sensual, cheerful manner and put fresh flowers by my bed.

I now have conversations with my old unfriendly thoughts about men, and I am ready to let go of my fear of being around or with a man.

Affirmations Regarding Negative Past Experiences

1. I forgive myself for _____ (fill in particular negative past experience).

2. I am now free of the past regarding my emotionally negative sexual experiences. I now focus on the value I learned from them.

3. I no longer focus on the losses I have suffered in the past. Instead, I hold on to those things that are of value to me.

4. My early painful sexual experiences do not make me a failure in sex.

5. Since I am responsible for my actions, I do not need to feel guilty about anything.

6. I now forgive women for their ignorant behavior toward me. I am no longer angry at women. I feel loving toward all people. I do not need to get even with women any longer; I can let them love me.

7. I now forgive men for their ignorant behavior toward me. I am no longer angry at men. I feel loving toward them. I do not need to get even with men any longer. I can let them love me.

8. My bedroom and bed is a safe and pleasurable place to be.

9. My bedroom is no longer a place of punishment, deprivation, or restriction. It is a reward, a place for rest, relaxation, pleasure, and inspiration.

Love Is the Only Answer

What is your story about why you do not have love in your life?

What are you committed to be, do, or have in relation to love?

New Insights I Have About Myself

What have you learned about yourself since reading this book so far?

1. My self-esteem/self-worth is now better......

_____

2. I feel deserving because

_____

3. I am handling my disappointments about

_____

4. Life is a constant reaching out to learn and grow; "I have grown in the following ways":

_____

_____

5. Do you have a victim mindset? If so, are you willing to give up this role?

6. Are you grieving about someone or something?

7. Are you willing to let go past hurts and disappointments?

**Love is the Only Way to Eliminate Negativity
From Your Life**

Write down all the people or things in your life that have affected you negatively:

1.
2.
3.
4.

> *"If love be not the law of our being, the whole of my arguments falls to pieces."*
> ~ Gandhi

I find that there are basically two types of love in this world: real love and false love. Real love has a quality about it that makes our hearts instantly open and relax. There's a spiritual energy about real love that feels like we all have an infinite amount of time, joy, and energy to give away. Real love is the most healing feeling we can have. It has an abundance of trusting energy and an exquisite sensation of accepting everything in our lives. Real love gives everything of itself to life, never holding back. It gives fully without conditions, always thinking "How can I help?" instead of thinking "What's in it for me?"

False love, on the other hand, wants to be like real love, yet it has an egoic mask it is hiding behind. This mask can only think in terms of "What's in it for me?" and believes that this approach will give it happiness in the end. It chooses to help others out of duty, a feeling of "I have to", or an obligation. It believes that it is doing the right thing, yet is blind to the fact that through obligation it's not actually enjoying its life. This false ego-based love is missing out on a more honest, vulnerable, and selfless approach. It has nothing to do with generosity, appreciation, or real giving. It's energy comes from scheming, planning, wanting, wishing, and hoping that it manifests what it wants. It can only think about its own needs instead of what's best for the whole.

Deep down inside, all this false love wants is to find the source of real love. It's tired of being a fake and wants what is real and true. It's ready to stop hiding behind fear, insecurity, and selfishness. It wants to be free from constantly feeling less than enough. This false love means well, yet its mask unknowingly creates more feelings of separation which makes it even more unworthy of love. Once the ego finds the courage to remove the mask it's wearing, it can stop repeating its dull unfulfilling life and step out of its darkness and into the light.

Removing the mask we are wearing allows us to start loving those unlovable parts in others, which they also believe are not lovable. Doing this, we gain the ability to love those unlovable aspects within ourselves. From this selfless place of loving and accepting whatever is inside others, we inadvertently heal ourselves. We find a selfless quality of love that feels truly powerful, courageous, and patient above all. There is a natural inclination to be kind with everyone and give as much as we can without feeling depleted. This path is real freedom, as it unmistakably brings out the best in everyone, making their hearts open to sing.

"And still, after all this time, the Sun has never said to the Earth, 'You owe me.'
Look what happens with love like that. It lights up the sky."

~ Rumi

When we meditate on what real love is, we discover that which is unchanging and never dies. We stop being attached to what is not real and find out what is real. We discover that the mind is not in charge, and the soul actually is. Through meditating on the source of real love, we transcend the perpetual swing of good and bad contradictions in the mind. The hypocritical thoughts cease to occur, and we awaken to a reality that has no criticisms about what we do or who we are.

Real love is that genuine movement of our soul in action. It is the most powerful healing energy in the Universe that can instantly transform everyone and everything. It instantly liberates any fearful, revengeful, or negative energy we may be caught in. Real love turns every heavy personal issue that we're facing into one filled with a soft liberating lightness. The moment we open up our hearts to real love, we feel reborn, and a true magical alchemy takes place. Without this real love we are lost, and our busy lives feel like they are constantly falling apart as fast as we can put them together. With real love, we become the glue which holds everything together in its perfect place.

No matter whether we are battling with depression, anxiety, fear, or loneliness, this sweet soft healing force of real love is always there and alive inside of us. It arises in our heart naturally, with a simple patient request for it to come forth. By quietly asking real love to be more present in our lives, we will find that it spontaneously arises on its own accord. Love hears our thirsty call and beckons us to meet it at its deepest abyss.

By trusting in real love and making it our leading guide, we can relax about living this life. We are led to freedom each day, feeling the sweet surrender of our ego's grip that thinks life has to be a specific way. Life is not about getting all our personal needs met. There is something more important than obsessing about our own desires and fulfilling the desires of others. We are here to discover the deepest peace of our soul, find that unending state of gratitude and sacred appreciation for what is. With real love there is a sensation of always being guided towards this. We are innocently led on the perfect path to the highest destination and can feel that whatever we choose to do, we will be safe and provided for along the way.

At the core of your being you are *The Source of Love* itself. Your body is a natural loving machine which is designed to experience all the greatest pleasures in this world. It is a super sensitive vehicle that has magical qualities. When this body of magical love becomes the center of our lives, we start seeing the divinity that is all around us. We understand each moment holds the most perfect conditions and ingredients for our soul's highest awakening. There is no effort in making things happen in our lives; our highest manifestations naturally show up. We know we are all powerful beings who are fearlessly guided every single breath of the way. By realizing the source of love inside our hearts, we know that anything and everything is possible.

By allowing our hearts to be guided by gentleness, we discover the source of real love. The interactions we have with others become opportunities to evolve, heal, and rejuvenate ourselves. This love invokes us to live our greatest possible life and discover what it is our heart is truly after. When real love takes precedence over the ego, we stop hiding from life and start taking more risks to open up to others. We may allow ourselves to "fall in love" with someone and then later "rise in love" because we trust that the unconditional friendship of real love will always be there.

Real love is that missing sweet nutrient which allows our life purpose to sprout, blossom, and become fully self-realized. It's what makes your heart open, your mind, relax and the emotions deep enough so everything becomes crystal clear about why we are here. Real love teaches us by example what we are supposed to do with our time here.

By opening our heart to feeling the simple, soft, sweet, loving energy all around us each day, we will find a peace, compassion, and spiritual depth that satisfy our every human desire. With real love as our greatest guide, we naturally bring out the highest joy in others, which causes us to find even *more joy* within ourselves.

> *"This is love: to fly toward a secret sky, to cause a hundred veils to fall each moment.*
> *First, to let go of life and Finally, to take a step without feet."*
> ~ Rumi

Real love is always here, shining behind it all. It is easily accessed inside you from a truly open and surrendered heart. It's always available, whenever we need it. When we rediscover that love is our essential nature, our heart is transformed into a vessel of forgiveness that assists all of humanity, touching the lives of everyone we meet. The greatest miracle of all occurs. People can no longer be with us and remain stuck in their darkness. They must transcend their contracted state and can no longer hurt themselves. Their heart, yearn to find this real love as well and becomes a conduit for the greater freedom. They find infinite compassion, eternal patience, and stop demanding that things be different than what they are. They instead move naturally closer towards their own heart, finding the real path of joy, appreciation, and zero resistance.

Simply through loving all the different parts of ourselves, we soon discover that we are the source of real love. We stop entertaining the movies of the neurotic mind and no longer identify with our victim stories. We find it more appealing to focus on that sacred spark within us which is truly divine. The most enlightening experience of our lives is found through loving what is. Loving what is includes loving every aspect of ourselves. This self-loving experience is not about being self-absorbed or selfish, yet simply honoring and recognizing the real divinity inside. We are seeing the greatest truth there is to see, as we open to the nakedness about who and what we really are.

I invite you to take this moment of your life right now to relax about the greatest issue you're currently facing. Imagine this issue is showing up on a movie screen in front of you, and the screen is getting smaller and smaller. The energy behind the issue is shrinking, becoming less and less real. The movie becomes so small that you can no longer see it, and you feel it disappearing from your life. Breathe in this feeling of relief into your body. Let yourself feel what it's like to let it go, and let yourself love yourself instead of this issue. Let love be your guide, and trust that it knows the way.

Are You Afraid of Being Rejected or Loved?

1. Do you feel unworthy or undeserving of love and attention?

2. Did you get attention from your Mom and Dad?

3. Are you accustomed to being ignored by people?

Example; Try to expand on these words to express how you may have felt about a past situation or person in your life:

I was made to feel I had no value and felt not worthwhile

_____

No one listened to what I had to say……..

A 7-Day Plan to Open Your Mind to Love

DAY 1
Self -Love

You must love yourself before anyone will love you. Meditate on this thought for today. Sit quietly and close your eyes for 10 minutes; then write any reflections or thoughts that come to mind. If any thoughts come up during the day, write them on a sticky note and transfer them into your notebook before you go to bed at night.

DAY 2
Let Go All Fear

Let go all fear of the unknown.
Say, "I will breathe deeply and often throughout each day."

DAY 3
No One Hurts Me Without My Acceptance

Am I allowing someone to hurt me? When you practice knowing that YOU are enough, then the ego is not so easily snagged in its old game of never having enough. The ego's game is simply forcing you to go to the core of who you are and know that you are connected to the Spirit Source. When you stop and realize who you truly are, you instantly boost your vibration and feel empowered again. The ego is a desiring machine that is always wanting, wanting, wanting, and doesn't know what true satisfaction is. It is only through the heart that you can find this feeling of being enough. The day you can see that each experience in your life is a "spiritual experience" you will never have a problem again. Negative thoughts naturally cannot rise in the mind, and you only have positive thoughts about yourself, the world, and everyone in it. Through living with the knowing that you are connected to everyone in this world, you begin overflowing with energy and love.

DAY 4
Give Up Your Need to Be Understood or Accepted

Write your understanding of this and what you will do to implement this.

Day 5
You Are Worthy to Be Loved

If no one has ever loved you in your life, become the first person who does. Write your understanding of this and what you will do to implement this.

Love Affirmations

1 Love is who I am.
2. Love is eternal.
3. Love is everywhere.
4. I am love.
5. I am the love that I seek.
6. I am calling in my lover now.
7. I am love, I am love, I am love.
8. Love is all around me; I see it, I feel it, I speak it.

Day 6
Do You Have Issues With Abandonment?

Who abandoned or rejected you?

At what age?

Will you allow this act, by someone who may have been self-centered or self-absorbed to determine yourself self-worth or self-value?

Write your understanding of this and what you will do to change this.

Day 7
How to Find the Love You Need

We all crave and need love. We are starving for love and feel deprived and lonely without it. I will let you in on the secret to fill your inner void for love. The Love You Seek Is Inside of You. Start loving yourself to show others what kind of love you seek and desire.

Answer the questions below to help you identify what is missing in your love life:

What is your relationship like with men/women?

> Imagine for a few moments that you can see, feel and experience your ideal partner. What would this person be like?

> Can you imagine that you are best friends with him/her?

> How do you deal with negative thoughts about men/women?

Thoughts to Ponder

Maybe Spirit wanted us to meet the wrong person before meeting the right one, so that when we finally meet the right person we will know how to be grateful for that special gift.

Maybe when the door of happiness closes, another opens, but oftentimes we look so long at the closed door that we don't see the one that has opened for us.

Maybe the best kind of friend is the kind you can sit on a porch and swing with, never say a word, and then walk away feeling like it was the best conversation you've ever had.

Maybe it is true that we don't know what we've got until we lose it, but it is also true that we don't know what we have been missing until it arrives.

Giving someone all your love is never an assurance that they will love you back! Don't expect love in return; just wait for it to grow in their heart. But if it does not, just be content it grew in yours.

It only takes a minute to get a crush on someone, an hour to like someone, and a day to love someone, but it takes a lifetime to forget someone.

Don't go for looks; they can deceive. Don't go for wealth; even that fades away. Go for someone who makes you smile, because it only takes a smile to make a dark day bright. Find the one who makes your heart smile.

There are moments in life when you miss someone so much that you just want to pick them from your dreams and hug them for real.

20 LAWS OF SELF-ESTEEM

Ida Greene, PhD

1. Accept yourself confidently as you are.
2. Never do anything in private that you would not want the world to know.
3. Think the best and expect the best of yourself at all times
4. Become your own best friend.
5. Perform to the best of your ability in all your endeavors.
6. Put no other person before yourself, including your friend, child, mother, father, lover, husband, or wife.
7. Develop and nourish your inner self continuously.
8. Listen and be open to your inner promptings and follow your intuition.
9. Hold yourself in high esteem and accept that there is a larger force in the universe that operates independent of you.

10. Know that there is a force that keeps the universe together, and that all things are always working out as they should.
11. Think for yourself, trust your judgment, and make your own decisions.
12. Worry less and trust your decision-making ability.
13. Become a decision maker.
14. Be a mover and doer of goodwill for yourself and all of humanity.
15. Treat yourself with kindness, dignity, and self-respect.
16. Guard the words that fall from your lips. Make them words of joy, happiness, and goodwill towards all, including yourself.
17. Avoid comparing yourself to others.
18. Expect the best from all people at all times including yourself.
19. Constantly seek ways to improve yourself.
20. Strive towards excellence in all you do, say, and think.

Nine Universal Relationship Truths
Margot Zaher and Jafree Ozwald

The following words will assist you in creating heart opening, soul-based relationships throughout your life. This practice will empower you in more ways than you know. When you are connecting with others from this soul perspective, the Universal love energy inside you shines, and you become a brighter light for everyone and you enlighten this world. The secret is to know that every relationship you have does not exist "outside" of you, and that the core connection is always found evolving within you. So expect it.

1. Dwell on the idea of an infinite love that is within you now. Rest in the feeling that arises inside you; relax into this so deeply that it permeates your innermost being. This way you have found your Source of love, and you are free from relying on your partner for feelings of love and validation.

2. You have the unlimited power to manifest your ideal relationship at any time. Since you can shift your vibrational frequency at any time, you can manifest anything at any time, including the love of your life. By transforming the way you are relating and connecting to others, you create a vibrational field around you which allows you to be more intimate with yourself and your partner.

3. Your partner can never "complete" you because you are already whole. The longing for completion that you feel inside comes from being out of touch with your Divine Self.

4. You can never make anybody feel angry, sad, hopeless, defensive, or any other emotion known to mankind. You are responsible solely for your own emotional state that is arising for you now.

5. Your true Divine essence is love, and you are connected to the essence of this energy no matter what you think, say, or do. Your very essence is the essence of love and holds the vibration of love at all times.

6. Ego by definition is always focusing on its wants. If your partner rarely satisfies your ego's desires, it is because both of your egos are running the show. To satisfy your ego and your partner's ego return to focusing on the soul source of your being.

7. Gratitude for your lover is always there smoldering like warm embers in the core of your heart. All it takes is for you to consciously reignite the spark, and the flames of gratitude will grow.

8. Behind every "undesired" behavior you see in your partner is your misperception of the Divine. At the core of everyone is the

most beautiful divine essence that is perfect, peaceful, eternal, and loving in all ways.

9. The act of not letting yourself, love someone or be fully loved, is the cause of suffering and emotional pain.

The Rugged Roads of Life

Ida Greene, RN, LMFT, PhD

Life is an ever increasing spiral,
On the path to human perfection;
It matters not the hue of your skin,
The color of your eyes, nor the color of your hair,
For self-mastery is an inner process,
That happens each time you overcome an obstacle.
For no one can ever determine,
The depth of your learning experience,
So continue on your journey to overcome
Your stiffest challenges,
For no one will ever know, the depths of your overcoming.
Continue to strive for excellence in everything you do.
For the path to fulfillment and happiness is
The Rugged Roads of Life

www.idagreene.com

Chapter 6
Follow Your Passion To Find Love

The Universe and everything in it is perfect. One aspect of that perfection is that each of us has been given one or more talents/passions. When we express these talents, we are carrying out our role in the overall plan of the Universe. The Universe supports itself by encouraging each of us to fully and freely express our talents. If we want the support of the Universe, we must do what Spirit created us to do and that is to express our talents.

When we do that, we are encouraged by a feeling of comfort in our bodies. When we avoid doing that, we experience discomfort. In order for us to have a life that works perfectly, each of us must be doing in life what we were created to do and that is to express the talent or talents that are given to us to express. Our talents are gifts of the Universe. We do not learn a talent. Each talent we have been given is a gift that comes with the tools to express it perfectly. If we have artistic talent, we have all of the skills necessary to express that talent successfully.

We do not become better at a talent. We just gain confidence as we become more comfortable in expressing our talent more fully and freely. As we open ourselves, we surrender to the Universe and let "It" play through us. Expressing a talent is not a conscious mind experience. An artist or musician does not think about what colors or notes to select. When we let go of any sense of limitation, we become totally intuitive and allow the infinite supply of energy to flow freely through us. It is an experience of freedom and joy, not thought and effort.

When we release all limitations, extraordinary things happen. When we are expressing our talents and passions fully and freely, we experience perfection. If only we could take a pill that would release all of our negative thoughts and open us to the Universe and its infinite supply of energy, we would express ourselves with total magnificence. Then and only then will we experience the joy and bliss of following our passion. When we follow our passion we are more alive, more vibrant, we have a love sparkle that can catch the attention of the love partner who is right for us. And who is just waiting to connect their love with our passion which could be the same as their passion.

How to Find Your Passion

I am passionate about children, travel, and dancing. My life's work is counseling children. It seemed that I just had to go to Ghana, Africa. I felt compelled. On Thursday, May 17, 2012, I left for Accra, Ghana. I wanted to see the "Door of No Return" where all persons of African descent departed when they came to the United of America as slaves. My grandmother was a six-foot tall dark complexioned woman who always said she was a Watusi African from Ruwanda, Africa. I vowed that I would go to Africa one day to see my ancestors. I also saw a picture in a magazine of Victoria Falls in Ruwanda, now called Zimbabwe, and I wanted to visit there again since I visited in April 2009 with my cousin.

I was born with many gifts and talents and so were you. I am passionate about helping others. All of my life work and professional relationships have been about helping people love and appreciate themselves.

What is the legacy you want to be remembered for after you are no longer alive? Often this is connected to your greatness. Greatness is a natural state. Anyone can enter this state, because our greatness can provide us a lifetime of achievement and love for self and service to others. We are all at a certain level of greatness already. There is greatness in all of us. We are quick to point out the faults or weaknesses in ourselves and others, but we fail to point out our areas of greatness. Our greatness is sleeping inside of us, and we just may need to develop our potential. Another aspect of greatness is how we live our life, and how we give back to humanity. You need to look for how you can be great without focusing on the ego of yourself. These are a few things that can blind us to our greatness:

1. Having a sense of false modesty, or a sense of being, inadequate or flawed in some way.
2. Confusion about how to be great; our legacy is a by-product of our greatness.
3. Family expectations that you be "normal" rather than "be great".

As we walk around feeling like unimportant earthlings, we have to remember that our life has value and that our life serves a purpose to help someone in the world other than ourselves. We just have to reach out and allow the person who is in need of our special brand of love to find us and connect with us.

Jealousy is Not Love

Love is not jealousy.
Love is not need.
Love is not ownership.
Love is not hoarding.
Love is not clinging.
Love is not restricting.
Love is not prohibiting.
Love is not bondage.
Love is not slavery.
Love is not dependency.

114

Love is not possession.
Jealousy is not love.
Imagine a world without jealousy.

Love is a revolving door. It is the many chambers of yourself and your life. The heart is an open chamber that is always looking for ways to help you evolve spiritually, and we do this evolution through the mechanism of love. Love truly is a many splendored thing; It is exciting, it is thrilling, and love is captivating.

These are some steps you can take to empower yourself as you reframe your relationship strategies, beliefs, and outcomes.

1. Realize that it is not okay for your needs and desires to be ignored. Notice if this is what has happened in the past, and make a goal to correct the situation. Because you can find true love if that is what you truly want.

2. Recognize the recurring themes in your love life to get you back on the path to find true love.

3. Change your beliefs about yourself and your relationship habits.

4. Develop self-awareness. Know who you are and be your authentic loving self.

5. Stop being too busy focusing on other people, and make more time to focus on yourself and your love needs. .

6. Sit down with yourself and outline what is important to you. Identify the core values of your life for your family, health, career, and relationships. This will determine the decisions you make about who or what you want your love life to be or look like. Identify the any limiting beliefs you have about yourself in relation to love and decide not to accept them anymore. If you believe you have to be the caretaker and to

never nurtured in return, know that about yourself so you can release that belief and find a life partner who aligns with your new belief that you are worthy of attention and love. Write your values down in order of importance. Doing this will help you understand your priorities and recognize a partner who shares those key values.

7. Identify your needs for what you want in a relationship. It is okay to have needs, it is normal, and vital that they be recognized and acknowledged in order for you to be happy in love. Notice your needs for affection, openness, communication, consideration, commitment, and trust.

8. Know your relationship requirements and settle for nothing less. Perhaps you fooled yourself into thinking there is a limited number of possible partners, and that you have to take what you can get or be alone. Unfortunately, that kind of thinking is a limiting belief and a self-fulfilling prophecy. When you expect less, you get less.

9. Define what you want; figure that out and persevere. Trust that if you apply yourself you can get what you really want in your life. Remember, you must be able to say NO to what you DON'T want, to be able to say YES to what you DO want.

LOVE   FEAR

Coming from Love:	Coming from Fear
Responsibility	Victim
Pro-Active	Re-Active
Towards	Away from
Own Shadows	Defensive, Denial
Growth Experience in Life	Resist Change/Stay In comfort zone
Open/Vulnerable	Protected/Attacking
Ask for Help	Do it Myself

Joy/Bliss/Curiosity/Peaceful	Anger/Sadness/Shame
Abundance/Cooperation/Win-Win	Scarcity/Competition
Live in the Moment	Fear future/Hold onto
Empower/Mentor	Control/Dominate
Be of Service, Hear	Use Fix
Pain as sensation, information	Pain as suffering, Bad
Learn lessons	Withdraw/Punish
Connection	Isolation
Observations/Evaluation/Choice	Judgment/Control
Does it Work or Not?	Is it Good or Bad?
Is it Empowering?	Is it Right or Wrong?
I Could	I Should
Vision/Mission	Survival
Seek to understand/Compassion	Judge/Blame
Go Through Fear (conscious choice)	Fight/Flight (unconscious choice)
Grateful	Jealous/Envious/Needy
Intention/Surrender	Expectation/Attachment
Ask for What I Want	Manipulate

When you live your life aligned with your core values you will feel on track and fulfill one of your highest needs: for your life to have meaning. Be your authentic self. If you are able to identify your core values and limiting beliefs, you've taken the first step towards being your authentic self. Embrace your core values and overcome your limiting beliefs and voila! You will find that you are attracting like-minded people and automatically deterring those who do not belong in your life. You will have created space for the right person to show up.

Knowing what makes you "**you**" will help you recognize when you are acting to maintain a relationship in a way that goes against your grain. That self-knowledge will warn you when you act in opposition of your core values. It will also alert you when you are reacting according to limiting beliefs. When you notice either of these things happening, stop and remind yourself of your end goal: a committed long term relationship that supports, enriches, and warms you, and act accordingly.

Think of a time when one of your needs was not met in a relationship. Did you feel hurt, angry, frustrated, unappreciated, or something similar? Being aware of your needs and that they are legitimate will help you to know when they are not being met. Awareness will help you quickly recognize when and if you are slipping into your old familiar pattern of not caring for your own needs first. Changing the automatic response patterns you've developed over the years requires mental intervention and physical action.

You have the power to choose who, what, where, when, and how, and get the relationship you really want. Develop a dating strategy and act upon it. Set your dating GPS to get to the relationship you deserve, and then follow the steps until you arrive safely. When you catch yourself getting off course and falling into your old familiar patterns, stop and re-evaluate your dating or relationship plans for your life. When you go against the innate response of your learned pattern it will feel uncomfortable or unnatural, because it's been well practiced and is all too familiar.

With the help of a Relationship Coach you can break your old destructive habits of looking for love in all the wrong places. To have lasting love you must look inside yourself to become a whole person. No one wants to connect or be in relationship with an emotionally handicapped or incomplete person. Complete yourself, and you will be attractive to another complete person. It is critical that you know how you present yourself to others and to the world.

Do you present yourself as a weak, helpless person who needs someone to take care of her/him or do you show others your strengths? It is unfair to you and the other person if you present yourself as weak to attract someone and then let your strong self, show up after you are in a relationship. Do not highjack your character or integrity just to be in a relationship with someone. If you are true to your inner self, you will one day attract a man who is deserving of you.

Do not let yourself be pressured by time or things people may say to you. Some people are supposed to be in a relationship and some are not. Look inside yourself to see what is your life's, purpose and why you are here on the planet. I was not supposed to have children so that I could be a foster mom, an adopted mom, and to counsel the many children I now counsel.

Because, you bought this book, you are entitled to a complimentary 20-minute coaching session with me. Call today at 619-262-9951 to schedule your session with me or one of my staff. Remember, who you are is Spirit's gift to you, and what you make of yourself through talents and time on the planet is your gift to Spirit. Develop your gifts and talents so that you make a difference on the planet. The universe is waiting for you to show up in a loving, caring compassionate way

www.IdaGreene.com

"No one is perfect.. that is why pencils have erasers."
Author Unknown

"Lots of people want to ride with you in the limo,
but what you want is someone who will take the bus with you
when the limo breaks down." ~ Oprah Winfrey

The most I can do for my friend is simply be their friend.
~ Henry David Thoreau

Bibliography

Gottman, John, Cliff Notarius, Jonni Gonso, and Howard Markman. *A Couple's Guide to Communication*. University Press, 1977.

Gottman, John Mordechai. *A Couple's Guide to Communication*, Champaign Ill., Research Press, 1976

Greene PhD, Ida. *Self-Esteem, The Essence of You*, People Skills Internationa www.idagreene.com

Stuart, Richard. *Helping Couples Change*, New York, Guilford Press, 1980.

Tavris, Carol. *Anger: The Misunderstood Emotion*, New York, Touchstone F 1989.

About the Author

Dr. Ida Greene is a Life/Intuitive Relationship Coach, Motivational Speaker, Licensed Marriage, Family, Child Therapist, Ordained Minister, Registered Nurse, Travel Agent, and Author of 20 books. She is also a Reiki Energy Balancing Practitioner, NLP Practitioner, Actor, Certified Hypnotherapist, and founder of Center of Self-Esteem, whose mission is to end violence and abuse of women and children. She speaks and provides training on How to Successfully Negotiate Anything, Light the Fire Within You to Maximize Effectiveness, Conflict Resolution, and Cultural Diversity.

Dr. Greene received the NAWBO "BRAVO" award, "Best Humanitarian Campaign", Book Publicist of Southern California, Writers Notes Book Award for her book *Anger Management Skills for Children*, San Diego Business Journal, Multicultural Heritage Award, and Book Expo America Self-Publisher of the year award. .

She is a frequent radio talk show guest, and can be reached for Keynote or Motivational presentations. She was listed in the book *100 Plus Most Admired African Women in Literature*. Her coaching skills were highlighted in T. Harv Eker's Coaching SuccessTrac newsletter, and her article on Stress Management was published in *"ALL" Magazine*.

Dr. Greene coaches on her latest book topics "How to Be Alone Without Feeling Lonely" and "Looking for Love In All the Wrong Places". She also coaches adults and counsels children with Attention Deficit Hyperactivity and conducts Parenting Classes on this topic. She provides a free coaching strategy session and group and individual coaching by phone at 619-262-9951. Her books are available at www.idagreeene.com, Amazon, and Barnes and Noble.

ASK DR. IDA

Dr. Ida shares her magical strategies with people through lecture, workshop, seminars, training, and individual consultations. Dr. Ida is available as an Inspirational Keynote Speaker, Motivational Speaker, and Coach.

The goal is to help you move through the barriers that keep you from being your best in your personal and professional life.

She does Past Life Regressions, Angel Readings, and Reiki Energy balancing sessions by phone appointments.

www.askdrida.com
askdrida@idagreene.com
619-262-9951

www.ingramcontent.com/pod-product-compliance
Lightning Source LLC
Chambersburg PA
CBHW060545100426
42742CB00013B/2456